MW01296015

Love Hard

DISCOVER HOW GENUINE INTENTION
AND ACTION CAN TRANSFORM YOUR
ABILITY TO CHANGE THE WORLD.

JASON WREN

WESTBOW
PRESS®
A DIVISION OF THOMAS NELSON
& ZONDERVAN

WestBow Press books may be ordered through booksellers or by contacting:

WestBow Press
A Division of Thomas Nelson & Zondervan
1663 Liberty Drive
Bloomington, IN 47403
www.westbowpress.com
844-714-3454

Unless marked otherwise, all Scripture quotations are taken from the Holy Bible, New Living Translation, Copyright © 1996, 2004, 2015 by Tyndale House Foundation. Used by permission of Tyndale House Publishers, Inc., Carol Stream, Illinois 60188. All rights reserved.

Scripture quotations marked ASV are taken from the American Standard Version.

ISBN: 978-1-6642-2189-5 (sc)
ISBN: 978-1-6642-2190-1 (hc)
ISBN: 978-1-6642-2188-8 (e)

Library of Congress Control Number: 2021901924

Print information available on the last page.

WestBow Press rev. date: 03/16/2021

*To Stephen and LaDonna for teaching
me what it means to love hard,
To Jenn, who holds me accountable for it,
To Sam, Isaac, and Anna for inspiring me to do it,
And to the many friends, family, co-workers, and others in my
life who give me the opportunity every day to get better at it*

Prologue

I wrote this book during the 2020 COVID-19 pandemic. As a hospital CEO, this was a hectic and trying time. It may seem strange to choose this time to write a book. But despite the controlled chaos of my professional obligations, I also found during the pandemic a desire to grow and learn personally. In turn, this personal growth led to new ideas and a willingness to lead others to new and better things.

2020 has provided many challenges. We experienced the once-in-a-lifetime (hopefully) pandemic, national and divisive debates about mask-wearing and other ways to combat the pandemic, social unrest in general, federal shutdowns, detrimental economic ramifications, new awakenings to racial disparities, and Black Lives Matter. There were protests to raise awareness of social injustice, counter-protests, rioting, highly divisive politics, a Presidential election which further expanded an already widening divide, Category 4 hurricanes, and even something called "murder hornets." People are angry. Angry at their circumstances. Angry at each other. Just angry. Given all the terrible things of 2020, our collective anger is understandable. But it should not be acceptable. There is a better way to relate to each other.

In the middle of every crisis, we can find opportunities if we are willing to look for them. As hard as 2020 has been for the healthcare industry during the pandemic, our organization has found so many opportunities as a hospital system to grow and improve. I've seen many situations of people stepping up to solve problems and help each other. There has been more time to grow personally, spend time with family, and develop new gifts, talents, and experiences.

One enormous opportunity provided by this year's challenges is to learn how to love each other rather than being so angry with each other. How to relate to each other better. How to engage with each other despite our differences. How to live more intentionally in our interactions and encounters, choosing to love each other well even when it's hard to do so. Even when we don't want to. Even when it's uncomfortable. Even when we'd rather walk away. We can and should intentionally choose to love hard. When we decide to put others' interests above our own and love them hard, the anger falls away. Tensions disappear. Restoration happens. And most importantly, when love prevails, a positive, lasting, and meaningful impact on the world around us happens.

2020 has provided ample opportunity to make the difficult choice to love hard and have an effect. There will be plenty of similar opportunities in future years, hopefully without the accompanying pandemic and murder hornets.

Chapter 1

LOVING IS HARD

*Love isn't a passive emotion but
an active, intentional choice.*

Loving is hard. At least it should be if we are doing it correctly. Most of us – and I include myself in this – often get it wrong because we have a fundamentally flawed understanding of what love is. In short, love is not about us or what we can *receive*, but about what we can *give* for others' benefit.

Google the word "love." The first two dictionary definitions of the noun form are "an intense feeling of deep affection" and "a deep romantic or sexual attachment to someone."[1] As a verb, it is defined similarly as to "feel deep affection for (someone)" or to "feel a deep romantic or sexual attachment to (someone)."[2]

These definitions are consistent with our typical understanding of love. We think of love in terms of how someone or something makes us feel, as a passive emotion that simply happens. But love should be active. Intentional.

It should be about our impact on others, rather than how we feel. Loving hard requires action and an outward focus.

Even though I know what loving hard requires, I, too, often don't do it very well. I can be selfish, focused on my feelings, my desires, and my needs. However, when I stop and pay attention to the world around me and am intentional about actively interacting with it and with others, a strange thing happens. I become more fulfilled, more joyful, more thankful, more positive, more gracious, more generous, more engaged, and more filled with what is good than when I try to feed and support my own feelings, desires, and needs. It may be harder, but the reward and impact are so much greater.

As a person of Christian faith, my foundational basis for this conclusion lies in the life and teachings of Jesus. However, the concepts can be applied, and indeed are applied, by people of all faiths and people of no faith. In fact, in my opinion, Christians miss real love and all it encompasses as much or more than anyone. I have failed in this regard many times. Nevertheless, while this book's purpose is not to evangelize my faith beliefs but instead to help all of us change our perspective of love, a discussion of the faith-based, foundational definition of love is necessary.

Before Jesus died, during the Last Supper with His disciples, He announced a new covenant with humanity, calling it "an agreement confirmed with my blood, which is poured out as a sacrifice for you" (Luke 22:20 New Living Translation, *You Version*). Shortly before the Last Supper, He told us how we should relate to each other under this new covenant in his attempts to explain it to His followers. "So now I am giving you a new commandment: Love each other. Just as I have loved you, you should love each other. Your love for one another will prove to the world that you are my disciples" (John 13:34-35). Even earlier, when asked about the most important commandment, Jesus replied,

"'You must love the Lord your God with all your heart, all your soul, and all your mind.' This is the first and greatest commandment. A second is equally important: 'Love your neighbor as yourself'" (Matthew 22:37-39).

He makes it sound so easy. Love God. Love others. This sounds simple enough, right? It may be simple to understand, but it is tough to do if we do it correctly.

Jesus himself showed us how hard this type of love is when he willingly died on a cross. And over and over again, throughout the New Testament, we see a discussion of love, which is much different than our understanding of love as the way something or someone makes us feel. Here are a few examples:

> Love each other with genuine affection, and take delight in honoring each other. (Romans 12:10)

> The commandments say, "You must not commit adultery. You must not murder. You must not steal. You must not covet." These – and other such commandments – are summed up in this one commandment: "Love your neighbor as yourself." Love does no wrong to others, so love fulfills the requirements of God's law. (Romans 13:9-10)

> There is no greater love than to lay down one's life for one's friends. (John 15:13)

> We know what real love is because Jesus gave up his life for us. So we also ought to give up our lives for our brothers and sisters. (1 John 3:16)

> You have heard the law that says, 'Love your neighbor' and hate your enemy. But I say, love your enemies! Pray for those who persecute you! (Matthew 5:43-44)

> Share each other's burdens, and in this way, obey the law of Christ. (Galatians 6:2)

I love the movie *Wedding Crashers*. The Owen Wilson and Vince Vaughn characters may have a misperception of what love should look like, but the movie is downright funny. There is a scene in which these two characters are crashing a wedding and make a bet as to whether the scripture reading will be from First Corinthians or Colossians. Owen Wilson's character confidently bets on First Corinthians. He wins, and Vince Vaughn's character pays up. You are probably familiar with these verses from weddings you have attended, either as crashers or, preferably, as guests:

> Love is patient and kind. Love is not jealous or boastful or proud or rude. It does not demand its own way. It is not irritable, and it keeps no record of being wronged. It does not rejoice about injustice but rejoices whenever the truth wins out. Love never gives up, never loses faith, is always hopeful, and endures through every circumstance (1 Corinthians 13:4-7).

This type of love is not a passive feeling. It is active and hard, and it requires intentionality. It requires a willingness to submit yourself to others. Despite these deep-rooted examples in the Christian faith, many Christians miss this. Many others miss it also. We miss it because we are focused on ourselves and how we feel. But those Christians and non-Christians alike who have actively and intentionally practiced loving hard understand how powerful this type of real love is.

When my wife, Jenn, was pregnant with our youngest child, our oldest, Samuel, was six years old. One day, I noticed Samuel standing nearby during one of Jenn's episodes of morning sickness. He waited patiently for the vomiting to stop and then asked Jenn, "Mom, when you are finished throwing up, will you make me a sandwich?" This question and its timing seemed perfectly logical to Sam. As a six-year-old, we expect his primary concern to be his own feelings at any given moment. When he asked this question, his feeling of hunger mattered most, and his mother's physical condition was irrelevant.

While Sam's question may be the natural response of a six-year-old, those of us who are older should know better. We are supposed to be more considerate of others. I am sorry to say Sam's natural inclination to focus on his own feelings or interests, regardless of what is going on around him, comes directly from me. It is not quite as excusable for me in my thirties and forties as it was for Sam when he was six. Yet, this story reflects how I often behave. It may not be as obvious. I may have gotten better at disguising it as I have aged. But those natural inclinations are still there.

My job requires a lot of time and energy. I enjoy my downtime, such as watching the latest Netflix series, watching a ballgame, or reading a book. If I'm honest, I enjoy those moments far more than social interaction. It is how I unwind. When I am home in the evening or during a weekend, my natural preference is to be left alone so that I can enjoy some downtime. My family and friends, however, deserve more from me. They deserve my attention, my engagement, and interest. Because I love them, I want them to receive from me everything they deserve. To do this, I must be intentional. I must choose them and their needs over my natural inclination to be left alone. I may fail more often than I succeed, but I know this is what loving hard requires. To love them fully, I must choose to be active and intentional and submit my desires to their needs. The television show, or the ballgame, or the book are important self-care tools for me, but sometimes they need to wait so I can love others well.

One of my favorite bands is NeedtoBreathe. I discovered them over a decade ago and attend their concerts as often as possible. Luckily, I've successfully brainwashed Jenn and two of our three children into becoming NeedtoBreathe fans and attending the concerts with me. I am still working on the middle child. NeedtoBreathe has a song called "Hard Love," with lyrics revealing an active, intentional, hard love, one that requires self-sacrifice and submission, rather than a passive feeling. The song describes how part of you must die when you love hard. One particular line stands out: "It's not enough to just feel the flame; You've gotta burn your old self away." [3] Who wants to do this? It does not sound fun to "burn your old self away" or to focus on others instead of our own feelings, and it certainly is not easy. Throughout this book, however, I hope you discover how great the reward is when we do this, not just for those we love hard but also for ourselves.

Acts 4 Others is a local, charitable organization in my community. Later chapters contain more about Acts 4 Others' background. Still, for now, it is enough to understand it as an organization striving to meet the needs of people struggling to find or stay in a home by providing resources to stabilize their living situation and help them get out of the poverty cycle. Individuals apply for help, and then a face-to-face meeting occurs between the applicant and Acts 4 Others' representatives. Acts 4 Others representatives discuss the applicant's background and story and piece together the reasons they are where they are, and help them start dreaming about their possibilities. These meetings last 20 to 30 minutes, and there are often two or three a week.

For a couple of years, I attended most of these meetings. My attendance required me to leave my job once a week for about an hour. The meetings were rarely convenient, in the middle of a weekday afternoon. At times, I considered reasons and excuses for not attending, all of which consisted of some version of "I don't have time." But most weeks, I went anyway. Each meeting was different, and all were rewarding in different ways. But one stands out.

Two of us from Acts 4 Others met with a lady who had no place to live. She had a drug history, struggled to find a job, and had nobody to help her. We listened. We shared resources and options. We helped her dream a little. But we had no immediate solutions. We could not get her in a home or in a job immediately. It is a process. Despite presenting a plan requiring some work and effort on her part, her response is one I will never forget. As we stood to leave, she asked for a hug. The other Acts 4 Others worker and I both gave her a brief, simple hug. I am not a natural hugger, and there was nothing special about this hug, at least to me. But after the hugs, this lady was in tears. She said, "It's been so long since someone gave me a hug and believed in me."

It was not convenient for me to leave work for an hour to attend this meeting or the other meetings. In fact, it was often difficult to do so. It was hard. It required me to be intentional and choose to engage with these individuals actively, to try to give them a glimpse of hope. A simple hug from this lady reminded me of the impact we can have when we love hard.

Chapter 2

HARDER THE LOVE, GREATER THE IMPACT.

*Sometimes we make the correct
choice to love hard. When we do,
the impact is meaningful and lasting.*

Love is active and intentional. I believe most people agree with these basic concepts, regardless of faith background. Love requires us to submit to others, to put others' needs and wishes above our own. As much as we want to do those things, it is easier said, or thought, than done. It is hard.

Our love has an impact on the world and the people around us. How much of an impact, and whether it is positive or negative, depends on whether we choose to love hard. Loving is hard mostly because our own needs and desires creep into our emotions and impact our decisions. When we love based on others' needs and desires, our ability to make a positive impact on this world has no bounds. Two recent interactions between Jenn and me demonstrate how this works.

Jenn and I had a disagreement recently. We were talking about summer travel plans for our family, which had been altered by the 2020 coronavirus pandemic. I like change, and once my mind has moved on to something new, I see no need to continue to think about it. It's time to act. Our initial summer travel plans were no longer possible, so, in my mind, it was time not only to discuss but finalize our new plans. Jenn, on the other hand, does not like change. She needs time to process and adjust to new ideas. Even though we agreed our prior plans were no longer feasible, she strongly disagreed with me on the need to decide on new plans at that moment.

As is often the case, in hindsight, Jenn was correct. There was no reason why we needed to decide or even continue discussing our modified plans right then. Even though Jenn knew the initial plans could not happen, she needed to process the change. We have been married for 20 years. I know this about her. I knew it during this recent "discussion." To love her well, I needed to stop the conversation when it became clear she needed more time to think and adjust. I failed. Why? I knew what was required, but my own desire to finalize plans, make decisions, and move on won out. My desires trumped what Jenn needed from me.

It's easy to pursue what we want or need. It's hard to pursue what someone else wants or needs. But the impact is so much greater when we take the more difficult path and love hard. My disagreement with Jenn is a simple example. Letting my desire to decide about a summer vacation days or weeks before it truly needed to be decided dictate how I interacted with Jenn had no positive impact. Instead, it reminded Jenn how selfish her husband could sometimes be, which has lasting negative consequences. What if I had practiced loving hard instead? Upon recognizing Jenn needed time to process our change of plans, I could have stopped talking. I should have stopped talking. Or better yet, I should have actively told Jenn how I recognized this was a change in plans she needed to process and to let me know when she wanted to discuss other options. This simple yet vastly different approach would have communicated to Jenn that she, and her needs and ways, matter. Even when I saw no need to wait, simple patience would have had a lasting, positive impact on our relationship.

In another recent situation, I got it right. (It may not happen often, but it happens.) A few days after the disagreement, our family ordered take out. The restaurant did not deliver and is about 10 minutes from our house. My son picked up the order and brought it home. We put the food on the table. I sat down, picked up my silverware, and started to eat. Then Jenn looked in her container. The restaurant had given her the wrong order.

I know how much she likes her go-to selection at this restaurant. I thought *I should drive to the restaurant and pick up Jenn's correct order.* Then I thought, *If I do, my food will get cold, and I'm hungry right now!* The restaurant is 10 minutes there and 10 minutes back. I wanted to stay and eat. But I decided to love hard and go pick up the correct order. This time, I made the correct choice to put Jenn's desires ahead of my own. When we decide to love hard, the impact is meaningful and lasting.

Loving hard is simply that – a choice. It is not a feeling. Like other choices, it is active and intentional. These two examples reflect typical interactions between most married couples. They demonstrate the frequent, minor situations which regularly arise in our relationships and interactions with the people around us and during which we have an opportunity to choose. In the first, I chose poorly, and Jenn felt devalued. I hurt someone for whom I care deeply. In the second, I chose well, and Jenn knew she mattered.

I have a close friend and mentor named Todd. Todd and I practiced law together for several years. I have received so much more from my friendship with Todd than I've given because Todd is one of those people who is excellent at loving hard. He's far better at it than I am. Todd cares deeply about people. He sees value and potential in a person, even when they do not see it themselves and even when their lives have not yet shown any evidence of it.

Todd played football for one of the most storied and successful college football programs in America. He loves sports. He loves to be around sports. He loves to talk about sports. (Actually, Todd loves to talk about anything, including topics other than sports, about which he knows very little but pretends to know a lot.) He likes to tell stories, even if you've heard them before.

Todd uses his love for sports to love people and have an impact. Todd has two daughters and no sons. Even though his daughters never played football, Todd coached pee wee football for years. He coached teams of different ages, from third grade to sixth grade. He chose to give away his time to other people's children because he understands what it means to love hard. He no doubt taught them much about how to play the game because he knows the game well. Just ask him. However, his impact on their ability to play the game was minor compared to his lasting impact on their lives beyond football.

He spent time with the kids away from practice and games. He talked to them about schoolwork. He held them accountable for their grades. He talked to them about treating each other well and thinking about others instead of themselves. He asked them to do something for their moms. Parents of some of those boys have shared stories with me about the lasting impact Todd had on their and their children's lives.

Often, although Todd only coached them for one pee wee football season, his relationship with them continued for years. Most school years, Todd created a mentor group with three or four high school boys who had played on his peewee team years earlier. Throughout the year, Todd would meet with those boys regularly. He took them to dinner, including at five-star restaurants to give them new life experiences. He met with them informally. He called them and checked in on them. Having been on the receiving end of many Todd phone calls, I am certain those calls lasted far longer than was necessary. Nevertheless, they were meaningful. He talked to them about things high school boys experience and encounter, about which they were comfortable talking to Todd but maybe not to their parents or family members. He took them to sporting events, paying for their tickets. During their time together, Todd re-emphasized and nourished the seeds of the lessons and teachings he had started years earlier during a peewee football season. During the next school year, he did it all again with a new group.

I listened to these mentoring groups' stories in awe, wondering why high school boys were willing to spend time with an adult. The answer lies in the way Todd loved them. It was genuine. It was authentic. Todd received nothing in return. Those boys knew this and recognized how much they benefited from the wisdom they received at a young age.

Listening to Todd describe those times leads you to conclude it was easy. I know Todd enjoyed it. But I also know it was not easy. It required him to spend time away from his family, away from his job, and away from his friends. He spent his own money on people who were not related to him, choosing to love hard because he knew the positive impact he could have. I have seen some of those boys interact with Todd years later as young adults. Their deep respect for him is evident. Because he chose to love hard, Todd's impact on them was deep, meaningful, and long-lasting. It required effort. It required intent. It required time. It required action. Although he received nothing in return, I'm certain Todd would tell you it was all worth it.

We choose every day how to use our time, how to spend our money, and what we speak to others. We can choose to spend them on things we find gratifying personally, which make us feel good, at least temporarily. Sometimes this is okay, and I am not suggesting that doing things for ourselves or our own benefit should never happen. But to have a real and lasting impact, a world-changing impact, we must get outside ourselves and spend our time, money, words, and actions on others, even when it does not benefit us at all. This is loving hard.

Most of us want to leave a lasting impact. Maybe I am naïve, but I believe this. If I'm correct, why do more people not love hard? Usually, our own personal comfort prevails. This comfort takes many different forms. Sometimes it is as simple as letting our own needs or desires control our decisions. Sometimes it is outright selfishness. Sometimes it is laziness. Sometimes it is a desire to avoid conflict or tension. Sometimes it is based on excuses, such as lack of money, time, or skill. All those things, though, are merely different ways of saying we prefer to be comfortable. But real impact happens along the harder path.

Think about a story where you or someone you know or heard about has caused a real impact. I am willing to bet the hero of the story left their comfort zone and actively and intentionally took hard action for someone else's benefit, with little or no benefit in return.

So it comes down to this: Do we want to be comfortable or impactful?

For many of us, this choice is driven by our faith. C.S. Lewis once said, "I didn't go to religion to make me happy.

I always knew a bottle of Port would do that. If you want a religion to make you feel comfortable, I certainly don't recommend Christianity."[4] Whatever our motivation, if we are willing to be uncomfortable and stretch ourselves in ways that push us to love hard, each of us can impact this world in positive and lasting ways.

Chapter 3

IMPACT ON PERSPECTIVE

Our world and our lives were changed
for the better because individuals
chose to set fear aside and love
each other, giving rise to hope.
Perspective makes all the difference.

Our perspective shapes our worldview. It is the lens through which we see the world, and we are all operating with our own unique lens. Perspective impacts everything we do and every component of our lives. And our impact on this world, positive or negative, is born from our perspective.

Perspective is defined as "a particular attitude toward or way of regarding something," or "a point of view."[5] It is not what we see, but the way we see it or experience it.

There is a scene in *The Great Outdoors* where John Candy's and Dan Aykroyd's characters sit on a porch, staring across a lake at undeveloped, hilly land covered in trees. John Candy speaks of his memories of the lake as a child and his desire to pass those memories to his children. He tells Aykroyd to look around at the "beautiful country" and take in the natural beauty. Aykroyd then begins a lengthy, detailed description of his view of the "underdeveloped resources" of several states, a "syndicated developed consortium exploiting" forest products, a paper mill and a mining operation, and a "greenbelt between the condos on the lake and a waste management facility." He goes on and on and then asks Candy what he sees. "I just see trees," he tells Akroyd.[6]

They are both sitting on the same porch, looking at the same lake and same undeveloped land. But what one sees is vastly different from what the other sees because their perspectives significantly differ. They view the world from different lenses.

My oldest son Samuel went on a double date a couple of years ago. He and Garrett, a basketball teammate, took two girls to dinner. Garrett is also Samuel's cousin. My branch of our family could be described as quiet and reserved. Samuel fits that description. Garrett's branch of the family cannot be described that way. They are outgoing and boisterous. They like to talk. A lot. Garrett is no exception. When Samuel came home after the date, I asked how it went. He said, "It went well, but Garrett wouldn't stop talking. I couldn't get a word in." A few days later, when talking to Garrett's mom, she said, "Garrett said the boys had fun on the date. But Garrett said Samuel didn't say much so Garrett had to carry the conversation." I shared with her Samuel's perspective, and we laughed at this story's perfect reflection of how the two family branches differ in their natural tendencies. The story also reveals how perspective works. Samuel and Garrett were at the same dinner with the same people. But their perspectives were entirely different.

Our perspective is typically based on either fear or hope. Other perspectives exist but mostly flow from one of these two base perspectives. A fear perspective results in fear of change, fear of rejection, fear of the unknown, fear of failure, fear of death, and fear of differences, such as things, people, or places we are not familiar with, or we do not understand. The fear perspective is inward-focused. We fear the many negative circumstances which could happen to us. In turn, our thoughts and decisions become consumed by this, even though we have little to no control over those circumstances or the harm they could bring. Because we are focused inwardly, we fail to make a positive impact on others.

But something remarkable happens when we intentionally choose to love hard, despite our fears: Our perspective changes. Potentially harmful circumstances do not disappear. They are always present, and there is a real possibility the harm we fear may happen even when we choose to love hard. We may be rejected. Change and difficulties may occur. We may not know what is going to happen. We may experience something different or new, and outside our comfort zone. But when we choose to love hard and focus our lives outwardly toward those around us, those fears don't seem to matter as much. We begin having a positive impact, sometimes in small ways and sometimes in grand ways. As this occurs, we develop a perspective of hope.

Although the possibility of bad things happening to us still exists, the positive impact of our outwardly focused love helps us overcome our fears. We see the good our actions can bring when we are intentional and active. We see what happens to those whose lives we are changing and the impact they then begin to have. Our outward focus changes the world, sometimes one person at a time. This results in hope – hope for good in the middle of a world full of difficulties and struggles.

I have a friend who is full of hope all the time, at least every time I have had a conversation with him. He deals with struggles and challenges, but one would never know it by talking to him or observing him. He is always positive and cheerful. He is encouraging and considerate. He has a smile on his face every time I see him. He goes out of his way to bring cheer and joy to those he encounters. And in perhaps his greatest accomplishment, his actions and words always seem genuine.

I love this friend, but he is not normal. He is the exception. A wonderful exception, but an exception nonetheless. Most of us move back and forth between the two base perspectives of fear and hope. As much as I would like to be like my friend, I am not. Unfortunately, nobody would describe me the way I have described my friend. There are times when this description applies to me, but there are plenty of times when it does not. There are times when I am moody and inward-focused. During those times, I miss opportunities to bring hope to others.

Most of us do not embrace one of these perspectives exclusively. Sometimes our perspective is rooted in fear. Sometimes it is based on hope. Often, our perspective shifts over time, from life season to life season. Sometimes our perspective shifts more frequently, from hour to hour or even minute to minute. Regardless of what is happening in our personal lives, we must repeatedly choose to love hard to impact others positively. When we do, our perspective follows.

During the 2020 COVID-19 pandemic, our children suddenly found themselves learning remotely and online. The pandemic began in mid-March during their spring break. For the first couple of weeks, the new schooling arrangement felt like an extended vacation. One of my children even declared a couple of weeks into the pandemic, "No school and pass/fail classes – this coronavirus thing is working out well for me so far." By early May and almost two months of online school, isolation, and limited social connection with friends, his perspective had changed. Instead of excitement about staying home, the same child now declared how much he missed school, words I never thought I would hear him say.

We can decide what perspective to have, but instead, we often let our circumstances determine our perspective for us. During the pandemic, one of my children's teachers provided examples of these opposing perspectives within a couple of days of each other. Jenn and I and our student received an email one day from this teacher to his honors students and parents. The teacher was frustrated by the struggles of online learning and teaching. Most of these honors students were turning in their work, but some were not. Those submitting the work chose many different digital formats in which to submit it. The teacher could open some formats but not others. His time was consumed by attempts to convert the not-so-accessible formats or track down assignments from students who had not submitted anything.

His frustration reached its limit. He fired off an email. Let's call this Email #1. In Email #1, he criticized the students for making his job more difficult. He commented how "ridiculous" it was that he needed to remind honors students to turn in work and use an accessible format. He suggested the students were possibly not as strong as their honors status would suggest.

I do not blame him, and many of his statements in Email #1 were accurate. I cannot imagine the difficulty teachers everywhere faced during the pandemic. Mid-week when the pandemic escalated, they were asked to suddenly start teaching in an entirely new way to students who had minimal incentive to study or work hard. I would have mailed it in, and I am so thankful for teachers like this one who continued to push students and demand good work during challenging circumstances.

I am also grateful he provided me such an appropriate example of perspective. Although I empathize with him and agree with the substance of his points in Email #1 even though there may have been a better style and tone, this email was borne of a negative perspective. He was frustrated. His circumstances were difficult. He was concerned about his ability to successfully teach the students in this new environment. He was losing precious time. This inwardly focused perspective on his own feelings and circumstances resulted in an action – Email #1 – which likely had little positive impact on its recipients.

But this teacher is a good teacher. He recovered well. Two short days later, we received Email #2, which revealed a changed perspective. The frustration and inward focus were gone, replaced with words revealing his love for his students. Email #2 was encouraging and uplifting, asking his students to relax and acknowledging the difficult situation they all faced. Instead of focusing on his own circumstances and challenges, with Email #2, he chose to focus on his students and recognize the pandemic's impact on them. His words in Email #2 demonstrated his desire to love his students well. Email #2 had a positive impact on students and parents alike. His choice to love hard gave rise to a new perspective, which in turn brought hope and encouragement in the middle of difficulty.

This story encourages me because it reminds me that my failure to choose well in the past has no bearing on my ability to choose well today and tomorrow. I may have had zero or negative impact yesterday. But that can change today. I can choose to shift my focus from myself to others, love hard, change my perspective, and as a result, change my world.

I am the CEO of an approximately 2,000-employee hospital system operating in north Texas. When the 2020 coronavirus pandemic began, our organization's initial reaction was one of panic as many questions without clear or easy answers arose. How do we make sure our employees are protected as they care for these patients? Do we have enough personal protective equipment? Do we have enough beds and ventilators? Do we have enough healthcare workers to take care of an influx of sick patients, especially if some of those workers become sick themselves or require isolation because of exposure?

As we worked to prepare for the pandemic and answer these questions about employee and patient safety, new questions about financial sustainability quickly arose. To preserve beds, staff, and equipment, we made the decision to suspend elective and non-essential procedures and surgeries. A few days later, the suspension became a statewide mandate. We had no idea how long it would last. Hospitals typically do not make a profit on sick patients admitted to the facility's medical or intensive care units. Instead, elective surgeries and outpatient procedures are the financial lifeblood of a hospital. Profits are minimal in the hospital industry, but what little profits there are come from these surgeries and procedures we now found suspended during the pandemic. Those profits, in turn, allow hospitals to provide less profitable or even unprofitable services necessary to care for sick patients.

Faced with the loss of our profitable service lines for an unknown amount of time, new fear-based questions arose. Do we need to furlough or reduce the hours of employees in the departments where services are not currently being provided or those not needed to support the frontline departments? Should some departments and services be suspended altogether? What other costs can we reduce to make up for the lost revenue? Is there anything we can do to help the employees directly affected by these decisions? How long can the hospital system survive without its most profitable service lines?

There were no good answers to any of these questions. In reality, we had very little control over most of them. We had a decision to make as an organization: Were we going to let a perspective of fear control our actions, attitude, and decision making? Almost immediately, I saw our organization answer this question with a resounding no. These healthcare workers chose to love and to love hard. The term "healthcare worker" includes nurses and physicians but also other clinical aides, technicians, therapists, social service workers, and pharmaceutical and laboratory staff, in addition to non-clinical support staff providing facilities, dietary, environmental, supply chain, revenue cycle, accounting, marketing, communications, human resources, and other non-clinical services.

They loved our patients by putting themselves in harm's way to make sure patients had the best chance to recover. They loved each other by serving the organization in new and different ways outside their regular departments. They arranged new and creative ways to feed staff members most directly affected by the pandemic. They made signs and wrote words on windows and sidewalks to encourage each other. They loved the community by hosting food pantries.

And in turn, the community loved us. Community members and organizations brought food almost every day to feed our workers. They held a community pep rally to cheer healthcare workers coming and going during shift change. They frequently texted, emailed, and mailed words of encouragement and support.

During the middle of the industry's most trying time, people chose to love hard. This choice resulted in a changed perspective. The questions causing the initial fear required answers, and we answered them as best we could. Fear occasionally crept into our consciousness throughout the pandemic. But mostly, from day-to-day and moment-to-moment, by choosing to love hard, a perspective of hope rose to the surface. Hope in each other. Hope in the future. Hope in the opportunities to become a better organization born out of a crisis we would have preferred not to encounter.

The positive impact of this better perspective is long-lasting. We learned how to trust and depend on each other more. We learned how to collaborate to solve challenging problems. We learned how to care for each other in more real and tangible ways. We learned how our words and actions of encouragement matter and truly make a difference.

These were the same people who experienced real fear because of a scary situation. With a changed perspective, however, those same individuals made a positive impact on our lives. Our very existence changed for the better because individuals chose to set fear aside and love each other, giving rise to hope. Perspective makes all the difference.

From which perspective – hope or fear - are we going to choose to operate today and tomorrow? Our impact and ability to change the world depends on that choice. How, many ask, can we possibly choose hope with so many terrible things happening in the world? We do not need to look far to find places in the world where war is being waged or other atrocities are being committed. In 2020 alone, a pandemic shut down the entire world and killed tens of thousands of people. Millions more lost jobs and suffered indirect consequences. In the United States, arguably the most advanced country in the world, school shootings occur regularly. Racial tensions remain despite decades-long battles to eliminate them. Poverty and all its consequences are nearby. Some ask whether things have ever been so bad. And how, they wonder, can we have hope.

It is true that we live in a world full of challenges, difficulties, and struggles. But it has always been true, and it will always be true. In 2016, we experienced the Zika virus and more racial tensions. North Korea tested the H-bomb. ISIS ravaged its way through the Middle East. Decades earlier, during 1968, the Vietnam War waged, and Martin Luther King, Jr. and Robert F. Kennedy were assassinated. From 1958 to 1962, a famine in China killed millions. During the 1930s and early 1940s, the world experienced a world-wide war and Holocaust, during which millions more died. From 1929 to 1939, 13 to 15 million Americans were unemployed, and half the banks failed during the Great Depression. We can find similar awful circumstances, no matter how far back we look. During the mid-1300s, a plague throughout Europe killed approximately one-third of the known population. In the 1100s and 1200s, people murdered innocents in a misguided attempt to advance their religion during the Crusades. The list goes on and on.

If we rely on the circumstances around us to determine whether we have hope, we will never find it. History has proven this to be true. Instead, our circumstances will most often result in a perspective of fear, making us afraid of what others think of us, afraid of getting sick, afraid of what might happen if the political party with which we disagree wins, afraid of failure, and afraid of whatever circumstance or situation our minds can imagine.

Alternatively, we can choose to focus our actions and efforts on those around us and love hard no matter our circumstances. From this perspective, we learn to live in hope, knowing that no matter if or when bad things happen and difficult circumstances over which we have no control arise, we will still care for each other. How we handle and address every conversation, event, and circumstance matters greatly, and in turn, the impact we have on the world around us will be determined by the choice we make.

There will be difficulties. But will we respond in fear

or with hope and love? During the middle of trying times and situations, the choice we make in how we respond and interact with others will have a real and lasting impact. Our choice to love hard from a perspective of hope can transform fear to courage, hopelessness to hope, restlessness to peace, and sadness and brokenness to joy.

In the book *God's Politics*, Jim Wallis tells one of my favorite stories demonstrating the world-changing impact we can have when we love hard from this perspective:

> The former South African archbishop Desmond Tutu used to famously say, "We are prisoners of hope." Such a statement might be taken as merely rhetorical or even eccentric if you hadn't seen Bishop Tutu stare down the notorious South African Security Police when they broke into the Cathedral of St. George's during his sermon at an ecumenical service. Desmond Tutu stopped preaching and just looked at the intruders as they lined the walls of his cathedral, wielding writing pads and tape recorders to record whatever he said and thereby threatening him with consequences for any bold prophetic utterances. They had already arrested Tutu and other church leaders just a few weeks before and kept them in jail for several days to make both a statement and a point: Religious leaders who take on leadership roles in the struggle against apartheid will be treated like any other opponents of the Pretoria regime.
>
> After meeting their eyes with his in a steely gaze, the church leader acknowledged their power ("You are powerful, very powerful") but

reminded them that he served a higher power greater than their political authority ("But I serve a God who cannot be mocked!"). Then, in the most extraordinary challenge to political tyranny I have ever witnessed, Archbishop Desmond Tutu told the representatives of South African apartheid, "Since you have already lost, I invite you today to come and join the winning side!" He said it with a smile on his face and enticing warmth in his invitation, but with a clarity and a boldness that took everyone's breath away. The congregation's response was electric. The crowd was literally transformed by the bishop's challenge to power.[7]

Choose love. Choose the hope perspective. If you do, your ability to change the world for the better is limitless.

Chapter 4

IMPACT ON FAITH

*Our faith should be nothing more than
love expressed over and over. It is
not easy and requires great sacrifice
and submission to others and their
needs. In fact, this requires more of
us than simply following some old
rules and laws because it requires us
to love others hard with nothing in
return for everything we do and say.*

Jenn and I lived on the East Coast for a while during our mid-20s, shortly after we were married. We were both raised in Christian families but in churches vastly different from each other from a denominational and doctrinal standpoint. These different backgrounds made finding a church to attend as a young married couple quite interesting. We shared basic beliefs and had much more in common than we may have realized at the time, but the differences stand out the most.

Jenn preferred one music and worship style. I preferred another. Jenn had a certain expectation about the teaching. I had the opposite. I wanted a church where I was comfortable, where I could make my faith fit my agenda.

One church we visited offered a "discovery class" one Sunday after regular services. The class was designed for newer attendees to answer their questions and give them a more in-depth understanding of the church and its beliefs and practices. This was in the middle of my skeptical and wandering years. Honestly, those years may have never ended. It is part of my nature. I remember questioning the pastor about his position on dinosaurs and how they fit within his understanding of the creation story in Genesis. I have since progressed in my faith journey and become convinced of two things. First, a few basic truths of my faith are necessary and non-negotiable, such as the life, death, and resurrection of Jesus and his command to love God and love others. Second, it is fine for people of Christian faith to differ on most everything else. I have reconciled many of my personal questions by studying and reading the different perspectives of people smarter than me who have researched these topics in greater depth. Other questions remain unresolved and unreconciled, yet I am content, hopeful, and joyful in my faith without being able to answer every question. I am content with others disagreeing with my conclusions on various topics or even disagreeing with my belief that we cannot answer some questions.

However, during my dinosaur discussion with the pastor, I conducted a litmus test, and he failed it. This was only one of many litmus tests I conducted back then. I had a box and needed my church to fit perfectly within it. In hindsight, I recognize how arrogant I was. But I simply was not comfortable with the differences. I was drawing lines in the sand all over the place based on my view of faith.

Our natural tendency is to expect our faith to benefit us. We often ask, what am I getting out of this church, or this speaker, or this music, or these people in my faith community? Loving hard requires a different approach to faith. Instead of approaching faith with a mindset of passively receiving, loving hard mandates a more active approach focused on what we can share with and give to others. For those of us who consider ourselves to be people of faith, choosing to love hard may have more impact on our faith and how we express it than any other component of our lives. It is also incredibly difficult.

We have been exploring how choosing love, the active and intentional kind of love, results in a positive, world-changing impact. Why then is faith's impact often so negative and divisive? My Christian faith is based on the most extreme act of active, intentional, outwardly focused love ever recorded -- the story of Jesus's death on a cross and subsequent resurrection. Some reading this book may not believe this event happened, or that Jesus did it willingly, or that He was who He said He was. That's okay. I can empathize. A large part of my early faith journey was overcoming skepticism, asking questions, and studying many different viewpoints before becoming convinced that my faith's foundation is true. But that's a story for another day. For now, we can hopefully operate under the premise that the type of hard love I'm writing about in this book is the same hard love on which the Christian faith is based.

Why do people who claim to be followers of the Christian faith so often not follow this example? We attend church on Sundays, expecting only to receive. Did the music today make me feel good? Did the preacher inspire me? How did they greet me? Were they friendly enough? What kind of opportunities are they creating for me to serve, as if we have no ability on our own to be proactive in our service? What type of youth and children programs do they have? Are my children enjoying themselves, or are they bored? Do I agree with everything they said, sang, and did this morning?

In short, we make it about us. Then, when we leave the church building, our faith often becomes a tool we use to draw lines in the sand, something I've frequently been guilty of myself. Rather than being the driving force behind our daily decision to love hard, faith too frequently becomes our justification for not loving at all. Sometimes it even becomes our justification for our hatred. We decide not to spend time with a person or those people because we disagree with their choices or how they are living. Their decisions or lifestyles do not match our faith principles, so we walk away. We choose not to go to certain places because we disagree with what happens there. We opt not to engage in critical conversations or issues because the other person sees things differently.

So many people of faith have a black and white view of the world. We want things to be in one bucket or another and not blend between the two. We view others as either with us or against us. We view questions as having one clear, correct answer, with all other answers being wrong. We believe there is a right side of an issue (our side) and the wrong side (the side of anyone who disagrees with us).

Are the lines so clear and distinct? Do you recall my friend Todd from an earlier chapter? He plays a regular game of putting people in one of two buckets. There are mountain people and ocean people but not people who like both. There are families who play games and families who view game-playing with great disdain. Some people open presents on Christmas Eve. Others consider opening gifts before Christmas Day to be sacrilegious. In Todd's world, the list of dividing buckets goes on and on. It is quite entertaining when he shares his newest revelation about the new categories he has identified. As much as I hate to admit when Todd is correct, I believe he is on this. On so many topics, so many of us fall into one camp or the other.

One of his favorite ways to categorize people is whether they are mercy-minded or justice-minded. When we encounter a wrong, most of us naturally lean toward feelings of mercy or justice toward the wrongdoer. Todd has correctly identified me as a member of Team Mercy and Jenn as a member of Team Justice. Those of us on Team Mercy are more willing to offer second chances or look the other way when wrongs occur. Those on Team Justice seek fairness and, well, justice in these situations. There are pros and cons to both approaches. But we all naturally lean one way or the other. Neither group is entirely right or entirely wrong. These inclinations, however, divide us.

I have another friend also, coincidentally, named Todd. (I promise I do have a handful of friends not named Todd. Maybe we will talk about some of them later.) This Todd is one of my closest, longtime friends and is also part of our hospital system's administrative team. To distinguish the two, let's call this one Hospital Todd and the other one Lawyer Todd. A few months ago, Hospital Todd and I discussed Lawyer Todd's views about Team Mercy and Team Justice. Hospital Todd is typically a member of Team Mercy. But a few days after our discussion, a situation arose involving a service provider with whom our hospital works. After listening for a few minutes to Hospital Todd rant about the situation and advise me on what he believed I needed to do to this particular service provider, it became clear it is possible we can move back and forth between Team Mercy and Team Justice depending on the topic or group of people at issue.

Back to Lawyer Todd. My response to his accurate observations of our natural inclinations when it comes to mercy and justice is to attempt to balance the two. If I become aware of my natural lean toward mercy in a situation, I find myself consciously attempting to shift toward justice, seeking equal parts of each in my response. Even this balanced approach, however, misses the point because it still draws a balancing line in the sand between the two. The best response is not to try to balance or equalize justice and mercy as if they are two competing forces but instead to recognize both may be fully and wholly appropriate and *consistent* responses to the same situation. Rather than balancing the two, I should fully embrace both. Instead of approaching a wrong as if we need to choose between mercy and justice, the answer usually is both, not either/or.

When it comes to faith, we have historically been more comfortable drawing lines in the sand than accepting and embracing our differences, even though this is what loving hard requires. I should pause here to make it clear I believe in basic truths such as the historical accuracy of the death, burial, and resurrection of Jesus. This, after all, is the sole basis of my faith. As Christians, however, rather than letting this fundamental event unite us, we let everything else divide us.

There are several reasons for this, but perhaps the most prominent is our failure as Christians to fully embrace what we refer to in our faith as the New Covenant. For those unfamiliar, here is a quick summary. The Hebrew scriptures, which Christians call the Old Testament, records a covenant between God and the Israelites. Specifically, God promised the Israelites he would free them from oppression and rescue them from slavery; he would be their God and claim them as his own people; and he would bring them into the land he promised to Abraham, Isaac, and Jacob and give this land to them as their own possession (Exodus 6:6-8). Additionally, if the Israelites obeyed God and kept His covenant, they would be his "own special treasure from among all the peoples on earth" and his "holy nation" (Exodus 19:5-6).

This was a covenant between God and Israel's people after they were freed from slavery in Egypt. It was made at Mount Sinai with Moses as the mediator between God and the Israelites. After making the covenant, God then gave them the Ten Commandments and hundreds of other laws and rules recorded throughout the Hebrew scriptures, all designed to protect them from outside influences and set them apart from other nations. It was a performance-based, ritualistic, legalistic system with which the Israelites had trouble complying. I do not blame them. I don't believe any nation could have complied with so many laws and rules, which is why this covenant included an animal sacrifice system to atone for sins. After this covenant was made, most of the rest of what Christians have termed the Old Testament is the story of God's chosen people struggling and failing over and over again to keep their part of the covenant and God's faithfulness to the Israelites despite their struggles.

Hundreds of years later, during the Last Supper with his disciples shortly before his arrest and execution, Jesus announced a new covenant. He took a cup of wine and announced "the new covenant between God and his people – an agreement confirmed with my blood, which is poured out as a sacrifice for you" (Luke 22:19-20). The writer of Hebrews described the new covenant as follows: "When God speaks of a 'new' covenant, it means he has made the first one obsolete. It is now out of date and will soon disappear" (Hebrews 8:13).

This new covenant is between all people and God, with Jesus as the mediator. Instead of physical prosperity, land, and protection, the new covenant promises hope, peace, and joy. Instead of requiring humans to comply with hundreds of laws and rules and make animal sacrifices when they fail, Jesus keeps the new covenant for us and made one single sacrifice covering us permanently. Instead of being for a specific people at a specific place and time in history, the new covenant extends to everyone for all time. The rules and laws of old are no longer needed to set us apart and protect us from outside influence.

This should be great news. The ritualistic and legalistic system of rules and laws is obsolete, replaced with something new. The works and performance requirements of the old are replaced with grace. God's relationship with us is different now. The hundreds of laws and commandments are replaced with the two we discussed earlier. Love God. Love Others. So simple but so difficult to do.

The Hebrew scriptures in the Christian Old Testament serve an important role in the Christian faith. They provide a historical context for Jesus and what he did. They provide insight into who God is. They give us great stories of faith and people of faith. They provide valuable lessons and teachings and help us understand the implications of what Jesus did.

The covenant found in those scriptures, however, and the rules and laws created under it are obsolete. Obsolete is a harsh word, but it's not my word. It's the word used by the writer of Hebrews in the New Testament. As Christians, though, instead of putting all our energy into loving God and loving others, we still use those old laws and rules to draw lines in the sand. Instead of loving hard under the new covenant, we use the old rules and laws to justify actions and words, often reflecting something quite different than loving others. We move back and forth between the two covenants, picking and choosing which of the old rules and laws we believe are still applicable today and which are not.

Under the old covenant, the rules and laws are what set God's people apart from other nations. Under the new covenant, Jesus said, "So now I am giving you a new commandment: Love each other. Just as I have loved you, you should love each other. Your love for one another will prove to the world that you are my disciples" (John 13:34-35). Today, as people of faith, we should be set apart by our love, not old rules and laws or our ability to follow them. We live in a performance-based society focused on achievements and successes, which is hard on us when we make mistakes. In this context, it is easier to understand and apply old rules than to love and offer grace. But by taking this easier path, we miss so many opportunities for our faith to have a world-changing impact.

Recent data shows a rapid decline in religious affiliation and church attendance among Americans. Eighty-four percent of the Silent Generation (born between 1928 and 1945) and 76 percent of Baby Boomers describe themselves as Christians. For Millennials, about half (49%) describe themselves as Christians, 40 percent as no religion, and 10 percent as a member of a non-Christian faith.[8] Similarly, 35 percent of Millennials attend religious services at least once or twice a month compared to 60 percent of the Silent Generation, 49 percent of Baby Boomers, and 46 percent of Generation X.[9]

I suspect there are many factors contributing to these statistics. Parents of younger generations may be less likely to take their children to church. Politics and societal changes have contributed. As Christians, we often point to this type of data and claim the world is changing for the worse. But we fail to identify what is likely the number one contributing factor, which is *us* and our failure to love hard in a new covenant kind of way.

We may be making an impact, but it doesn't appear to be positive. One 30-year old millennial living in a southern U.S. city described his and his wife's decision to withdraw from the faith this way: "My family thinks she convinced me to stop going to church, and her family thinks I was the one who convinced her. But really, it was mutual. We moved to a city and talked a lot about how we came to see all of this negativity from people who were highly religious and increasingly didn't want a part in it."[10]

They haven't necessarily stopped believing. They just do not want to associate with us because instead of loving others well, many people of faith have become negative, critical creatures. I am speaking generically. I know there are also many exceptions. There are many people of faith who love God and love others expecting nothing in return and no matter if others deserve it. But these numbers reveal we, collectively, are missing it. The fruits of the new covenant – grace, love, hope, and joy – are attractive. If people do not want to associate with those things, then we are likely the problem.

Bob Goff is a lawyer and author who has written two books on how to love people well. I love how he has described these concepts:

> We tell people to "come as they are," but only if they'll change enough to make us comfortable once they arrive. That's not how love works. Love says we need you even more if you're different from the rest of us. Love says everyone has something to teach us, and God will use people from the edges to expand our understanding of His grace right in the middle of where we live. Love says everyone who's invited is truly wanted.
>
> We're meeting people at the starting line, not the finish line. We shouldn't say everyone's invited if we're going to act like they're not welcome when they come.[11]

I won't revisit them here but look back at the different verses about love discussed in Chapter 1. Our faith should be nothing more than love expressed over and over. It is not easy and requires great sacrifice and submission to others and their needs. In fact, this requires more of us than simply following some old rules and laws because it requires us to love others hard with nothing in return for everything we do and say.

Instead, as I used to do in those early days of marriage when we were searching for churches, and I was asking pastors about dinosaurs, we try to make our faith fit our view of the world, or our view of what is right, or our view of how people should act. Rather than letting our faith and these simple yet difficult commands to love God and love others drive all we do, we use our faith to drive our personal agendas. We are great at using our faith to justify our non-loving actions and our complacency. I have certainly been guilty of this.

But as I have learned to simplify it to loving God and loving others and loving them hard, I've become more comfortable with not being comfortable. The church we attend now often makes me uncomfortable, which is a good thing. I do not agree with everything said in every sermon given. I do not agree with all my co-churchgoers' politics or faith perspectives, including others in church leadership with me. I have been one of as many as five elders of this church. On many topics and questions, we would likely have five different answers if asked our position. I love this. There are disagreements and tension but also respect and trust despite our different perspectives. It is uncomfortable, but it challenges and stretches me. But it is so much better for growing and advancing my faith than being in a church where everyone agrees with me, and there are few differences in backgrounds and perspectives. I hope everyone reading this finds an uncomfortable church to attend.

When it comes to faith, this is what loving hard looks like. It is uncomfortable. It is tolerant of differences and opposing positions on issues. It requires acknowledging our personal preferences, understanding, and interpretations are not necessarily the correct way of looking at things. Often the situation or issue is gray and cannot be answered in black and white terms. Sometimes it does not fit perfectly in our box and may not make sense.

We people of faith often see ourselves as part of the accepted and enlightened group, judging, ignoring, and marginalizing those on the other side of the various lines we have drawn. Our faith is about us and what we can receive, waiting for whatever reward may await us in eternity.

What if we operated differently, looking for ways our faith can impact others instead of ourselves? Instead of drawing lines in the sand when people have a different faith-view than us, what if we loved them hard no matter their differing views? What if we embrace our differences and love each other despite them? Like justice and mercy, what if we understood the answer often is not either/or but both.

I believe the answer to these questions is this: world-changing impact would occur within our faith circles and within all our other circles with people outside our faith. It is possible to love people well despite major differences of opinion. Chester Wenger was a longtime pastor in the Mennonite Church. His son was gay, a lifestyle contrary to his church's teachings, and had been excommunicated from the Mennonite Church decades earlier. When Chester Wenger was 96 years old, Pennsylvania changed its laws and allowed Wenger's son to marry his longtime partner. They asked Wenger to marry them, and he agreed, knowing he would likely lose his pastoral credentials under Mennonite Church doctrine.[12]

In November of 2014, Chester Wenger wrote an open letter to his "beloved Mennonite Church." His letter revealed his deep love and respect for people on all sides of a hard situation and provided us a beautiful example of loving hard despite deep differences of opinion. He noted he was "profoundly reluctant to write this letter." He started with a description of his decades-long service to the Mennonite Church. After describing the wounds left by these painful circumstances, he wrote:

> The world we live in is no longer the idyllic Eden. It is a broken, complex, messy, violent, and yet wonderful world. God's mercy-filled grace infuses our broken world with goodness that keeps surprising us with joy – and healing. God's grace also calls us to faithfully love God and neighbor above all else.
>
> ...
>
> When my wife and I read the Bible with today's fractured, anxious church in mind, we ask, what is Jesus calling us to do with those sons and daughters who are among the most despised people in the world – in all races and communities?
>
> What would Jesus do with our sons and daughters who are bullied, homeless, sexually abused, and driven to suicide at far higher rates than our heterosexual children?
>
> ...
>
> My dear wife, Sara Jane, and I love all of our [eight] children. We give thanks for the remarkable Kingdom work each of them is

doing. We know that several of our children believe that the church should not endorse same-sex marriage. And several of our children believe that same-sex marriage is a faithful and godly choice when blessed by the church.

While the tension around this issue is painful in our family, we continue to love each other, to sing, to pray, and play together. Our children all honor us with deep devotion and faithful care – and genuinely enjoy each other.[13]

He noted his shifting views over the years on same-sex marriage and his and his wife's personal wrestling with the question, and he encouraged his church to genuinely consider the issue. When he reported his decision to preside over his son's wedding to church leaders, "they responded with grace-filled pastoral listening, while acknowledging that what I'd done was out of step with established" Mennonite doctrine and terminated his credentials. In a remarkable show of respect and love for all involved, Chester Wenger said, "I am at peace with their decision and understand their need to take this action. I know persons will accuse me of my transgression, but my act of love was done on behalf of the church I love, and my conscience is clear. My dear companion of 70 years and I declare our enduring love for the [Mennonite Church] and all God's people. We carry no bitterness or regret for our actions. Our hearts are filled with love for all. *We pray that our love in family and Church will bind us together in God's family even when our understandings of God's will may differ.*"[14] (Emphasis added.)

I never met Chester Wenger. I do not know how his letter was received by the Mennonite Church or its impact on its intended audience. But his decision to love everyone involved despite deep disagreement and differing views of a highly divisive issue, and love them hard, has had a positive and meaningful impact on me. I suspect the same is true for others both within and outside the Mennonite Church who have since read his letter. Some will disagree and use his views to create further division. But I hope many others will use it as an example of how it is possible to love each other despite our differences. To love each other in the middle of deep disagreement and tension. If we can follow Chester Wenger's example of loving hard rather than continuing to draw lines in the sand, perhaps our faith can impact the world the way his letter impacted me.

Chapter 5

IMPACT ON IDENTITY

We are all here to leave a positive and lasting impact. We do this by loving hard. And when we figure out what it looks like in our individual lives and that our identity lies in the middle of this ability to have such impact, it is profoundly consequential.

How we view ourselves and what we consider to be fundamentally true about ourselves has a great impact on our actions and whether we fulfill our purpose. Identity and purpose are connected at the hip. We will consider purpose in the next chapter. First, we need to examine identity and what happens to our identity when we choose outwardly focused loving-hard lives. Our identity becomes clear as we discover our unique gifts and talents and use them to love hard. And as we use our identity to fulfill our loving-hard purposes, we, in turn, help others discover their true identities.

Let's start by looking at the various external circumstances and internal traits that partly form our identity or what we perceive it to be. Many people and circumstances in our lives influence our view of ourselves, but perhaps nobody has a greater impact on how we perceive our identity than our parents. This impact can be positive or negative. Sometimes it results from parents actively involved in our lives, either positively or negatively. Sometimes it is the result of our parents' absence. Regardless of how they have made an impact on us, for most of us, our parents have played some role in our identity.

I have loving and caring parents. They remain active influences in my life today. Much of what I have learned about loving hard, serving others, and putting others' interests ahead of my own comes from lessons my parents have taught me. They created opportunities for me that others have not received. I recognize my good fortune in this and am so appreciative of what they have provided me.

Of course, like everyone, there are obstacles and some generational defects I have received from my parents as well, and those obstacles must be overcome. For example, on my mother's side, I come from a long line of people who can fix anything. My grandfather on my mother's side was as handy as they come. He could also build anything. He had more tools than anyone I've ever seen. He loved to fix things, and he was good at it.

My grandfather on my father's side was one of the kindest and most considerate men I've known. But when it came to fixing things, he had only one solution – duct tape. There was duct tape everywhere. If you had a problem with the television, duct tape was the solution. A hole in the roof? Try some duct tape. A broken piece of furniture? Duct tape. He put forth valiant effort to fix and improve things, but his sole method was duct tape.

My father has taken a different approach. He's not handy at all, but he pretends to be. He tries to help. He wants to help. But over the years, we have learned it's better not to ask him. When Jenn and I were newly married, we lived a few hours away from my parents. Once while my parents were visiting, Jenn's car had an engine problem. It was making a terrible sound. My dad wanted to help. He went outside, opened the hood, and asked Jenn to start the engine. He listened with a thoughtful look on his face. Then he offered his assessment. In his expert opinion, someone had dropped a tool down in the engine. It was loose and rattling around. He was certain the engine itself was fine, and we simply needed to find the loose tool. We thanked him and, after my parents left town, sought the advice of an actual expert. They found no loose tool but did find actual mechanical problems causing the terrible sound.

My handiness game is very similar to my dad's and his dad's. Specifically, I have no handiness game. I can't fix anything. I'm not even handy when instructions are provided. When Jenn and I got married, someone gave us a set of storage shelves. Unfortunately, they required assembly. Shortly after we returned from our honeymoon, I decided to impress my new bride and assemble our shelves. I laid out all the pieces on the floor and went to work. Hours later, the task was complete. The shelves were assembled. I simply needed to set them upright. When I did, we noticed a slight lean in one direction. Maybe it was more than slight. One leg was several inches shorter than the others.

Rather than pretend like my dad, I have accepted a lack of handiness skills as part of my identity, so I don't even try. I have a good friend named Karl. (See, I told you I have friends not named Todd.) Karl can fix anything. I now maintain a Karl list. If we notice something needs to be fixed, I add it to the Karl list. Once the list has four or five items on it, I call

Karl. Karl comes over and completes in a couple of hours what would have taken me two days. And all of Karl's shelves are evenly balanced when you stand them up.

Our families shape us and who we are. So do our friends, activities, careers, education, and geographical locations. All these circumstances have a profound impact on us. Some are good. Some are bad. But these external circumstances all shape us, as do our more natural, inner traits.

Jenn and I have three children – Samuel, Isaac, and Anna. They have vastly different identities. Some of their external circumstances have been similar. All three were fortunate to have Jenn as their mom and got stuck with me as their dad. Except for a couple of years when the boys were very young, all three have grown up in the same neighborhood, in the same house, in the same Texas town. The same extended family members in grandparents, aunts, uncles, and cousins are influencing their lives. Some of their external circumstances have been different, however. They have different friend circles. Samuel spent two and a half years as an only child. Isaac has grown up with an older brother. Samuel has not. Anna has grown up with two older brothers. They have grown up in the same household with the same parents, but their individual experiences have been different.

And perhaps most importantly, each is naturally unique and distinctive. Their personalities are different. Their interests are different. Their dreams are different. Samuel is the most chill, relaxed human I've ever met. Nothing seems to bother him. It is both his best quality and his most infuriating quality. Isaac, on the other hand, is passionate. He gets worked up. I love this about him. And it also drives me crazy sometimes. Why can't Samuel be more passionate? But I love his calm and relaxed approach to life. And why can't Isaac be more chill? Yet, I so appreciate his passion. Despite having two introverted parents, Anna is the most outgoing human I know. She never meets a stranger. She can have a thirty-minute conversation with a four-year-old or a seventy-year-old. She loves life. She says whatever she is thinking. Like some of her brothers' characteristics, this one is both Anna's strength and her weakness. She is only eleven right now, but she is vocal, independent, and confident, which is exactly the type of woman I want her to become.

On the other hand, she once asked her grandmother's friend why she was so old. When she was four, she and Jenn were on a pre-school field trip. Another mother had a baby in a carriage. Jenn asked Anna if she thought the baby was so cute. Anna responded, "No. That baby is ugly." We are working on teaching her that every thought need not exit one's mouth. It appears to be a lifelong journey. On the other hand, we do not want to squelch who she naturally is.

Samuel, Isaac, and Anna all carry the same last name. They are similar in some respects, but there are more differences than similarities. They each have their own unique identity with their own unique gifts and talents and their own distinct challenges and struggles for all the reasons discussed above. Despite their distinct identities, my desire for them is the same. I want them to know and understand who they are and have confidence in their unique identity. I hope they learn to listen to the stirrings in their hearts, which are helping to define their purposes. And I dream of the ways they will choose to love hard the world around them, using their unique identities and experiences, both good and bad, and as a result, shape their identities into individuals who have a lasting, world-changing impact.

Identity has a simple definition. It is the characteristics determining who or what a person or thing is, or a close similarity or affinity.[15] Our external circumstances and internal traits, such as the ones we have explored in this chapter, are part of what forms our identity. But so are the choices we make, especially concerning how we relate to others. How do we view ourselves? Is it as someone who receives from others or gives to and serves others?

We tend to view identity as something over which we have no control, based solely on external circumstances we did not choose or internal traits with which we were born. If we ask ourselves the question, who am I, what is our answer? We usually have multiple answers. I am whatever my last name is. I am what I do for a living. I am a husband or a wife, a father or a mother, a son, or a daughter. Perhaps the answer is based on our skills or abilities. I am an athlete. I am a musician. I am a teacher. I am a speaker. Our answer could be based on our successes and accomplishments. I am a survivor. I have overcome addiction. Often, however, it is based on our failures and flaws. I am an addict. I lost my job. I have made mistakes. The list goes on and on, and our answer to this question often changes over time. Sometimes we base our view of ourselves on others. We compare ourselves to others, sometimes elevating ourselves over others and sometimes wondering why we don't measure up. We envy what others have or have accomplished. We want their gifts and talents instead of recognizing we have our own unique gifts and talents and spending our time to embrace and cultivate them.

What we believe is fundamentally true about ourselves forms the reason why we believe we exist and forms our purpose. The wrong identity leads to false purpose. Therefore, it is crucial that we understand our true identity and that our choices play a vital role in our identity in addition to those external circumstances and internal traits over which we may have little control. When we love hard, we have a positive impact. When we understand our ability to make a positive impact based on our choices, our perception of ourselves changes. Our identity morphs from characteristics determined by others or our circumstances over which we have no control to choices we control. For all of us, the answer to the question of who we are and why we exist is found in some unique version of loving hard and impacting the world in a positive way based on our own distinct gifts and talents. How we go about it may look different for each of us, given our unique gifts and talents. But God has given us all the ability to do this. We are all here to leave a positive and lasting impact. We do this by loving hard. And when we figure out what it looks like in our individual lives and that our identity lies in the middle of this ability to have such impact, it is profoundly consequential. It not only shifts our perception of our own identity but also shapes and develops the identity of those on whom we are making an impact.

Our identity lies in this fundamental choice we have, to know God created us to use our special gifts and talents to impact the world uniquely. When we base our identity on our circumstances, it leads to a purpose based on those circumstances. If we perceive our identity as our job or career, then work becomes our sole purpose and focus. If we derive our identity from family or friend groups and relationships, our purpose often becomes to please people. If we identify primarily as a mother or father, our purpose follows. If our identity is based on any of our circumstances, our purpose becomes defined and limited by those circumstances. How we answer the identity question drives our focus and how we spend our time.

I'm somewhat embarrassed to admit I recently started watching *Downton Abbey* with Jenn. The show aired several years ago during the decade young children hindered our ability to watch television. With older and more independent children now, some of our own independence has returned. It's phenomenal. I highly recommend having older children.

Downton Abbey is nothing more than a soap opera, and I'm only two episodes in at the time of writing this. Despite heckling from both my sons for watching it, I've decided I like it. For those unfamiliar (spoiler alert), it is set in a fictional English country estate in a time period beginning in 1912, immediately after the *Titanic* sank. It depicts the lives of the aristocratic Crawley family and their domestic servants. Robert Crawley is the patriarch. He and his wife have three daughters and no sons. His heir to the Downton Abbey estate, a cousin due to Robert's lack of any sons, perished on the *Titanic*. Another more distant cousin becomes the heir.

Robert's identity is wholly and completely wrapped up in the Downton Abbey estate. He has no job or profession. As best I can tell after two episodes, he does nothing except have others dress him, have others serve him, and walk around admiring his massive estate. He inherited the estate and referred to it as his life's work. His sole focus during the first two episodes has been making sure whoever inherits the estate from him appreciates it as much as he does.

I understand Downton Abbey is a fictional story. But while watching the first two episodes, I couldn't help but wonder how many of us are like Robert Crawley, letting our circumstances or family name define our identity. And more importantly, I wonder how much opportunity to make an impact and change the world we miss when we become so focused on this false identity.

Our true identity is not based on such circumstances. Instead, our purpose should flow from our unique abilities to love hard and have an impact. Our circumstances and traits may shape this identity and are certainly part of it. In fact, we may be better at loving hard because of past failures and mistakes or because we have learned lessons the hard way. Ultimately, though, our choices are what define us and, specifically, whether we will choose to use those circumstances and traits unique to us to love hard and have an impact. Do we fully understand how equipped we are as individuals to significantly make an impact on those around us with confidence and an outward focus? When we are committed to loving others hard and see the immediate impact it has, we discover a new identity. Only once we understand our identity are we fully capable of fulfilling our purpose.

Now that you know who you are, what are you going to do with it? From false identity comes false purpose. But from true identity derived in our recognition of our unique giftings and talents and our choice to use those gifts and talents to love hard comes world-changing, life-giving purpose and impact.

Loving hard has a positive impact not only on the identity of the one offering love but also on the one receiving it. A few years ago, Acts 4 Others had an opportunity to work with a participant who was a young mother. When this mother came to Acts 4 Others for help, she had been drug-free for only 11 days. She was living in her car with no back window and a busted front window. In her words, she had "no self-respect, no self-esteem, and no friends." Child Protective Services had removed her daughter from her custody, and reunification with her daughter appeared unlikely.

According to this mother, Acts 4 Others gave her renewed hope. They put a roof over her head, paying all her expenses for the first two months. They helped her find a job. After two months, she started sharing in some of the responsibilities and paying some of the bills. After another couple of months, Acts 4 Others stopped paying expenses but stayed in contact with her. They helped her remove herself from an abusive relationship. Five months later, she was in a home for the first time in her life as the only person on the lease. She had a job and had replaced the windows in her car. She was drug-free.

In her words, she had "self-esteem, self-respect, and real friends she never dreamed of having." Reunification with her daughter had become a true possibility in five short months, and several months later became a reality. She commented how instead of pushing her away because of her addiction and circumstances, Acts 4 Others "loved on me, and that's what I needed. I needed love." She said, "I have one life to live, and I want to live it well."[16]

A group of people loved this woman hard and changed her life. In turn, her identity changed. No longer did she view herself as a homeless, daughterless addict or let her circumstances define her. With help, she chose her true identity as an individual with unique gifts and talents and her own ability to love others hard as she had been loved. With her daughter in her life once again, her lasting and positive impact on her daughter and others results from a changed and impacted identity.

Chapter 6

IMPACT ON PURPOSE

Sometimes to love hard, we must walk away from current circumstances and do something new. Sometimes we simply need to pay more attention to the world around us regardless of our circumstances and choose to be present and engaged. Whether globally in our careers or from moment to moment, the decision to love hard gives us purpose.

O nce we understand who we are, our ability to make a positive, world-changing impact has few limits. When we take the external circumstances and internal traits making up a portion of our identity and combine them with the powerful choice to love hard, then true purpose is revealed and can be accomplished.

Purpose goes far beyond what we do for a living, our circumstances, or the skills and training we have. Purpose relates to impact, and by choosing to love hard, our purpose and impact can be great. We all have this potential, regardless of whatever we may have believed limited and restrained us in the past. No matter our job or our circumstances, by choosing to love hard, we can live with purpose from moment to moment. But it requires us to have an outward focus in those moments and be active and intentional about loving hard.

It took me a long time to understand this, and truthfully, I still struggle with it. One of my best friends since eighth grade remains one of my closest friends today. We have a deep, authentic friendship allowing us to be honest with each other even when the truth hurts. Years after high school, when we were in our late 20s or early 30s, he told me what a snob I was in high school. I don't remember the conversation's context or why he needed to tell me this years later, but I remember his words and how he seemed to enjoy making me aware of others' prior perceptions of me. We also have the type of relationship in which some good-natured teasing can be fun. While it stung to hear him say this, it really wasn't a revelation. I had become slightly more self-aware by then and knew he was right about the younger version of myself. I was never intentionally a snob. I held no ill-will toward anyone as best I can recall. I know I always cared about helping others, even when younger. But I was rarely present in the moment. I was so focused on my future, or the next task at hand, or trying to achieve success in the classroom or athletics, I often failed to be present and intentional with those around me. This absence resulted in the "snob" perception.

As a result, I missed so many opportunities to love people hard and positively influence their lives. I missed my purpose in those moments. It wasn't due to a lack of care, but instead my failure to understand the importance of being present and intentional with those around me. From my standpoint,

I was simply taking care of my business and moving forward. From the perspective of those around me, as my dear friend found so much enjoyment in telling me, I was a snob. Those are moments, days, months, and years I cannot get back.

As mentioned, I still struggle with this. Ask Jenn, Samuel, Isaac, and Anna. Far too often, I am disengaged and distant. It's not because I don't care. It's simply because this is how my mind works. I'm overly focused on what needs to be done or on what's next. To stop and be present *and more purposeful* requires great effort and intentionality. But this effort is necessary to fulfill our purpose of loving hard and having an impact from moment to moment. Whether it's with our family, co-workers, or whoever happens to be crossing our path at any given moment, we need to stop, engage, and love them in the moment. When we do, we position ourselves to best fulfill our purpose.

Purpose is defined as the "reason for which something is done or created or for which something exists."[17] In other words, purpose equates to why. Why are we here? Why do we exist? The answer to these questions is similar for all of us and is, simply, to love hard and have a positive and meaningful impact. It's that simple. But it's hard to do. And how each of us goes about doing it will differ significantly and be driven by our identity and unique gifts and talents. But we are here, quite simply, to love hard and have an impact.

Once we understand who we are and what our capabilities are regardless of our circumstances or past, the question becomes, what are we going to do about it? Will we be content to sit back and spend our time making sure our needs are met? Will we focus on our own comfort? Will we keep our unique gifts and talents hidden from the world or use them only to benefit ourselves? Or will we choose to step into our purpose and do the things we were created to do by using our uniqueness to love hard in whatever moment or situation we may find ourselves?

Several months ago, I wrote a personal *why* statement. Businesses often do this to connect the dots between vision, mission, and strategy. It's equally important for us as individuals to develop our personal why. Specifically, by intentionally considering this and writing it down, it helps us connect the dots and bridge the gap between our collective why of loving hard and having an impact on how each of us will individually use our unique gifts and talents to accomplish our purpose.

I wrote, "To live a life that shines light into all situations, serves others, and leads those around me to something collectively greater than our individual selves." Even though I finally wrote these words down as a personal *why* statement only very recently, these concepts had stirred in me and driven most of my behavior and major decisions for years. Capturing these concepts in a short statement, however, forces me to be more intentional about fulfilling my purpose in a manner unique to me. It's a daily reminder of why I'm here. It provides a framework within which to make decisions. Some decisions may be large in scale, such as career decisions. Others may be smaller in scope, such as how I'm going to spend my weekend and with whom I will spend it. But both can be equally impactful if the decisions are driven by purpose and why.

What are different ways we can fulfill our purpose to love hard? In Chapters 5 through 7 of the Book of Matthew, Matthew describes Jesus's Sermon on the Mount, when Jesus laid it out for us as clearly as possible. You need not be a Christian to love hard and live with purpose or to do so in the way Jesus described, and I hope these passages provide some insight as you look for ways in your daily moments and interactions to fulfill your loving-hard purpose in your own unique ways.

During this sermon, Jesus teaches us to mourn when our circumstances require it and to comfort those who are mourning. We should both "hunger and thirst for justice" and be merciful. (Remember the discussion earlier about being full of both justice and mercy and not simply trying to balance the two?) We should be peacemakers. We should do what we know is right. We should be salt and light to those around us. We should not become angry with others. We should reconcile with those who "have something against" us and settle our differences. We should turn the other cheek. We should give others more than they need or ask. We should love our enemies rather than showing kindness only to our friends (Matthew 5:3-48). We should give freely, privately, and with joy rather than storing up treasures for ourselves. We should forgive those who sin against us. We should be content rather than worrying or wanting more (Matthew 6:1-34). We should refrain from judging others, especially because we all have our own issues. We should treat others the way we want them to treat us (Matthew 7:1-12).

How much different would the world be if we lived like this? What if we lived as peacemakers instead of creating discord in our relationships, families, workplaces, and with those who disagree with us or persecute us? Do we truly take care of the poor, or do we say things like, "They need to work harder; I worked for what I have, let them work for theirs." Are we equally hungry for justice while fully showing mercy? Are we salt and light making a positive impact on those around us, or do we simply blend right in with the rest of the world, content in our own comfort? How many of us, even (or perhaps especially) people of faith, live in anger at those around us, condemning and judging and expecting behavioral change instead of simply loving and extending grace to each other?

I understand this is not easy, and when I'm not intentional about doing these things, I fail miserably. This is why loving hard is so difficult and requires being actively intentional. But this is where our purpose lives. If we can live this way from moment to moment and interaction to interaction, fulfilling our purpose to love hard, we can all be world changers.

I spent years mistakenly equating purpose to job and career. Career is no doubt a tool which may be used to help us fulfill our purpose. And as we better understand purpose, I hope we will make career decisions that will best equip us to use our unique gifts and talents to fulfill our purpose of loving hard and making an impact. When I say I spent years mistakenly equating purpose to career, I mean I spent years viewing the job or career itself as the purpose rather than merely a tool through which we can fulfill our purpose, failing to understand the impact I could have from moment to moment.

The reality is all of us can live purposeful lives, loving hard those around us and positively changing the world around us, regardless of what our job is and regardless of our external circumstances. No matter what our job is -- whether we even have a job -- we have the opportunity every single day to love hard and make a difference using our uniqueness. It may be through a simple conversation or encounter. It may be through generosity or hospitality. It may be through action to serve others wholly separate from whatever we do for a living. Regardless of the job itself, we can love hard and positively affect the people with whom we are working. For those who don't have a job or are retired, the same opportunity presents itself with every interaction and encounter we have each day. Fulfilling our purpose is not dependent on job and career.

Many of us may never have an opportunity to have a

job or career we find fulfilling or that itself directly allows us to live with purpose. Sometimes it's necessary for us to take whatever job is available to help us pay the bills. But opportunities to love hard and make an impact present themselves to all of us every day, although we may need to look for ways to do this outside the daily grind of a job.

Even though all of us can do this regardless of our circumstances or our job and career, as we grow in our understanding of purpose and in our lives and careers, we can look for ways to use what we "do for a living" as a tool through which we can fulfill our purpose. For some, this may require a changed perspective of your current job or career. Perhaps your job has presented opportunities to you all along, but you have failed to see them or seize them. For others, the quest to love hard and live purposeful and impactful lives may trigger a job or career change. On the one hand, I've emphasized we can live intentional lives of impact and purpose regardless of job or career by being intentional from moment to moment and choosing to love hard no matter our circumstances. I also changed careers to have more purpose. This may sound like I'm contradicting myself, but both are true. We need not rely on our jobs or career to have purpose. However, if our situation allows, we can nevertheless choose jobs and careers to further facilitate our purpose and impact.

I'm a lawyer by education and background. I went to law school immediately after finishing my undergraduate education. After law school, I worked for the highest court in Texas for one year, then took a job with a large firm on the East Coast. After a brief time there, Jenn and I returned to Texas to start our family, and for the next decade, I worked for a few different law firms, eventually becoming a partner in one. During all these years, I never felt fulfilled and eventually changed careers. The main motivating factor in this career change wasn't money or geography but purpose and impact.

I need to make something clear before moving on with this story. I have great respect for the legal profession. My father spent over 35 years as a lawyer and is now a judge. My wife is a lawyer. Some of my very best friends and mentors are lawyers, including Lawyer Todd. All of them have lived purposeful, impactful lives, loving others hard, both separate from their careers and because of their careers. As with anything else, whether we lawyers live purposeful and impactful lives is the result of whether we choose to have an outwardly focused perspective and love others hard. I certainly had the opportunity to have purpose and impact as a lawyer and, at times, did. But I ultimately decided I could make an even greater impact elsewhere. My decision to change careers should in no way reflect on the positive and lasting impact so many of my family and close friends have had in the legal profession.

I will always consider myself a lawyer even though I no longer practice law. And I intend to maintain my law license in case current or future employers no longer have a place for me. But despite my great respect for the profession, and despite our ability to love hard and live with purpose regardless of job or career, my pursuit of opportunity to love hard and live a more purposeful and impactful life led to my decision to change careers. There were several things about being a lawyer I enjoyed. But I never could shake the nagging sense, which I believe was God's way of speaking to me, that I was meant to spend my precious time doing something else.

In 2013, therefore, I informed my law partners I had taken an in-house position as general counsel of a hospital system. Technically, I was still a lawyer, providing legal work and counsel to the hospital. But this was an opportunity to be more purposeful and intentional with my time. In addition to providing legal work, I was part of a leadership team tasked with making operational and management decisions to advance and grow an organization whose underlying mission is to care for people. We all have varying experiences within healthcare, some good and some bad. The healthcare industry is complicated. I joined an organization, however, whose primary purpose at a foundational level is to take care of people when they need it the most. To help them heal. To provide compassion and care. In short, to love them.

This foundational purpose drove my decision to change careers and eventually advance within the hospital organization. After a few years as general counsel, I somehow convinced the board of directors I was capable of additional responsibility, and they made me president and chief executive officer. I haven't looked back. I no longer have the nagging sense I should be doing something else. This may change at some point. But for now, my days and hours are filled with purpose. As can be true with any job or career, loving hard is found in the moments. It's in the relationship with my leadership team as we discuss strategy and vision and as I try to lead them to something collectively greater than our individual selves. It's in the daily interactions with employees and patients, which still require me to be intentional about stopping and being present in those moments to make sure I don't miss an opportunity to love hard and have an impact. It's in making high-level, strategic decisions with the objective of preparing ourselves to provide excellent care to our communities when they need us the most.

During my second year of college, one of my friend's parents came to town and took my friend and me to dinner. We went to the Old San Francisco Steakhouse. It was a welcome change from my normal fare at the university cafeteria or nearby fast-food restaurants. My friend's dad asked about my plans. I told him I was considering law school. His dad and brother were both lawyers, but he encouraged me to keep something in mind as I pursued a career. Whether as a lawyer or in some other profession, he advised me to "work on building something lasting and meaningful for the community." Those words stayed with me, and I thought of them when the career-change opportunity presented itself. I have the good fortune of leading an organization that, hopefully, has a lasting, meaningful, and positive impact on our patients, employees, and communities. Making a career change was not easy, and there were plenty of reasons to stay the course as a lawyer. But putting myself in a better position to love hard and have impact ultimately won out.

Sometimes to love hard we must walk away from current circumstances and do something new. Sometimes we simply need to pay more attention to the world around us regardless of our circumstances and choose to be present and engaged. Whether globally in our careers or from moment to moment, the decision to love hard gives us purpose. We are free and equipped to carry out our intended purposes today, no matter where we are in life. By having an outward focus and choosing to love hard every day, we care for and positively impact this world and the people around us. We are agents of positive change.

Our circumstances, experiences, and past, some good and some bad, shape and form us and give us those characteristics and gifts unique to us which allow us to love hard and impact our own unique ways. But we need to choose to use those things of the past to love hard rather than letting them hinder us in our pursuit of purpose. We can be free from those things binding us, but freedom is not simply removing ourselves from old things and no longer doing those things. It is instead using those things that shape us to do something great. It's not freedom from what holds us back but freedom for something new and impactful. I understand purpose better because I spent so many years not fulfilling it. But those past years and experiences cause me, even require me, to be so much more intentional and purposeful now.

N.T. Wright is an Anglican bishop who has written about purpose in the context of Jesus's resurrection and what it means for Christians, but his comments hopefully will help inform your purpose and help you choose to love hard to fulfill it regardless of your faith with the knowledge of how much impact you can have here and now:

> Jesus's resurrection is the beginning of God's new project not to snatch people away from earth to heaven but to colonize earth with the life of heaven. That, after all, is what the Lord's Prayer is about.
>
> The point of the resurrection is that the present bodily life is not valueless just because it will die. What you do with your body in the present matters because God has a great future in store for it. What you do in the present, by painting, preaching, singing, sewing, praying, teaching, building hospitals, digging wells, campaigning for justice, writing poems, caring for the needy, loving your neighbor as yourself, will last into God's future. These activities are not simply ways of making the present life a little less beastly, a little more bearable, until the day when we leave it behind altogether. They are part of what we may call building for God's kingdom. [18]

Are we simply living out our lives, trying to stay as comfortable as possible for as long as we are here? Making sure we and our children and family members are safe and taken care of? Complaining about how things are changing and about other people, expecting them to change? Judging and condemning those around us and longing for the good old days, whatever those were? Or are we instead choosing to be difference makers by loving hard and having an impact? As N.T. Wright explains, what we do in the present and whether we live purposefully right now has lasting implications for the future.

We need to be salt and light to those around us. When we fail to choose purpose, our light is faint. When we love hard, our light shines brightly. Each of us has a unique light that forms our unique purpose, and the world needs it to shine. May we all stop wasting our time on things we were not meant to do and stop living under the limitations of our circumstances or our past. Instead, may we choose purpose so our light may have a lasting impact for years to come. Drew Holcomb captures this brilliantly in his song "Good Light," in which he sings about how each of us has something positive and magical to offer the world. [19] I encourage you to listen to it, sing along with him, and then choose to live in the way captured by the song.

Chapter 7

IMPACT ON SOCIETY

*Loving hard makes an impact. We
cannot change society all at once.
But we can change society one
person or family at a time.*

Do you remember the *Friends* episode when Phoebe and Joey argue about whether a good deed can truly be selfless? Maybe you aren't a *Friends* fan. (I hear there may be a couple of you out there.) In case you are not familiar with the episode, Joey is on his way to co-host a telethon on PBS. He comments that this opportunity will give him "TV exposure" to help his struggling acting career while also doing a "good deed for PBS." Phoebe argues Joey is not really doing a good deed and is "totally selfish" for simply wanting to get on television. Joey pushes back, claiming "there is no unselfish good deed." He points to Phoebe's willingness to be a surrogate for her brother and his wife during their pregnancy. Joey claims even though it was a "really nice thing and all," it made Phoebe "feel good so that makes it selfish." Their argument ends with Joey concluding selfless good deeds don't exist and Phoebe promising to find one.[20]

I laugh every time I watch this scene. It's intended for humor, and it's funny. But it also reveals some truth about our motives, mine included. Too often, my service to others has been more about me. Joey has accurately captured what has far too frequently been my approach to good deeds. Certainly, I wanted to help people. But I cannot deny the existence of other self-motivating factors. It was expected of me. It was the trendy thing to do. It made *me* feel good about *myself.* Too many times, serving others was nothing more than me simply checking a box.

I went to college in San Antonio, Texas. My university was active in community service, and there was no shortage of opportunities to participate in service projects. Periodically, but not often enough, I would volunteer. One project involved serving overnight at a downtown homeless shelter. We went to the shelter around dinner time and stayed until the next morning. We handed out soap and towels. We cleaned. We did whatever other tasks the shelter needed to be done but could not afford to pay someone to regularly do them.

This was almost 25 years ago, and I still remember how I felt all night. Yes, I helped. Yes, I provided a service. Yes, I performed some good deeds. But mostly, I impatiently awaited the next morning when I could leave. When I could check this box as complete. My body was there, and it performed some menial tasks. But I wasn't truly present in the moment. I loved, but I didn't love hard. I didn't commit. I didn't fully engage. My impact, therefore, was far less than it could have been.

There are many other examples of this throughout my life—more than I would prefer to admit. I have served on boards, city councils, and other community organizations, all in the name of serving others. But in hindsight, I question whether my impact was as significant as it could have been because at least some part of my motivation was to make myself feel good and check a few boxes.

How much more difference can we make in the world around us when we put aside any benefit for ourselves and love others solely for their benefit? It is a subtle but significant mindset change. Society needs more of us to make this change in our approach to service and solving problems. The greatest societal challenges we face can best be addressed by people willing to love hard those around them. From homelessness to education to healthcare to every other aspect of society, our potential to play a role in solving these problems, even if on a small scale, one person at a time, relates to our willingness to fully engage with a focus on loving and impacting others. It cannot simply be about checking a box.

I am thankful for people like my friend Sheila, who has taught me so much about loving hard. Sheila is a registered nurse. She and I work for the same hospital system. Sheila regularly, almost annually, receives awards recognizing her as the best nurse in the county and acknowledging her caring and compassionate spirit. Those recognitions are celebrated by Sheila's co-workers and friends, usually without Sheila. She does not want the praise or the acknowledgment because she fundamentally understands it isn't about her. A couple of years ago we had an internal event to celebrate some of these recognitions. As I read through the names, I saw Sheila's. Before the event, I knew that when I called Sheila's name, she wouldn't be there. I was right. Sheila was too busy spending her time loving her patients to receive recognition for herself. She continues to make a lasting impact on the society within which she operates while expecting absolutely nothing in return.

As Sheila progressed in her healthcare career, she

transitioned from bedside nurse to a role we call "patient advocate." Nobody is better equipped to advocate for our patients and their needs than Sheila because nobody loves and cares like Sheila. Sheila would never admit it, but she works too much. She gives her cell phone number to every patient and patient family member with whom she meets. People call her for help 24 hours a day, seven days a week. And Sheila always responds because she cares more about those patients than herself. A few years ago, we decided to help Sheila set some boundaries to give her more personal time and time away from work. We bought her a cell phone. We asked her to use the work-owned cell phone to contact patients and protect her personal number. We suggested she set certain hours when the new work-owned phone would be turned on and when it would be turned off. You can imagine how well this went. Weeks later, we discovered the new work phone had never been used. We gave up and decided to let Sheila be Sheila.

Several months ago, I walked to the hospital cafeteria to get breakfast early one morning. I saw Sheila in the hallway and walked with her briefly to ask how she was doing. Without breaking stride or slowing down, she told me she couldn't wait to get upstairs and love on her patients. "They are the reason I'm here," she told me. It was clear I was slowing her down. It was far more important for Sheila to get upstairs and do her thing than to stop and make small talk with the CEO. I love and appreciate this so much about Sheila. I knew I needed to simply say thank you and let her go on her way.

Sheila is changing the world one patient at a time by loving them hard. She puts their needs above her own and expects nothing in return. I admire and respect Sheila as much as I admire and respect anyone. Through her simple actions and very few words, she is a living example of how a culture and society can be changed by loving hard.

In the previous chapter, we looked at how our purpose often has nothing to do with our job or career. In Sheila's case, the two match perfectly. But such a match is not necessary for us to make a difference. To impact society, we simply need to put our interests aside, get out of our comfort zone, and do something.

In 2008, there was a stirring deep within me to do something meaningful for my community during my lawyering years. Later, I changed careers and found more daily purpose in my new career. But this stirring was different and had nothing to do with a job or career. Something within me was pushing me to shift my focus outward toward the community around me. To use any skills or abilities I had to help others regardless of what I did for a living. Or better yet, to put together a group of people with giftings and abilities different than mine or better than mine to be intentional about meeting the needs around us. It's important to listen to these inner stirrings because purpose is often found in the middle of them and missed if we ignore them. It took a few more years of prayer and conversation with others to seek guidance and advice before I gained some clarity. But this stirring, which started in 2008, resulted in the creation of Acts 4 Others four years later.

Acts 4 Others has a simple vision to create a community and region where available resources are used to eliminate needs and improve the common good. Quite simply, the organization seeks to connect unmet needs with available resources. The organization pools resources from churches, individuals, and charitable organizations to fight the root causes of poverty. It facilitates various projects to accomplish this purpose. What started as a vague and foggy idea became an organized effort of 10 individuals to pay attention to the world around us and try to do something to address the problems we saw.

Acts 4 Others first targeted education. From a few conversations with local leaders of charity organizations, we discovered a roadblock for people in our area wanting to take the exam to obtain their General Education Diploma, or GED. The exam itself was offered and easily accessible, but the lack of a preparation course was a problem. Individuals who wanted to take the exam either chose not to because they were unprepared or took it but had trouble passing it.

These individuals had decided to drop out of school before completing high school. Sometimes this occurred because of their own poor decisions, and sometimes it occurred through no fault of their own because of external circumstances or others' decisions. Regardless, the failure to complete high school had limited their opportunities and became a root cause of the poverty they now experienced. One decision years earlier limited their job options and prevented further educational opportunities. Now, however, they wanted to make a change and obtain their GED to eliminate this root cause. In turn, new opportunities could be created, resulting in lasting impact on their own lives and their families and friends and their own circles and societies. Whatever happened in their past to cause them to drop out of school no longer mattered. They were ready to move forward, and they simply needed some help.

After some investigation, Acts 4 Others discovered resources already developed and present in the community through a grant program providing training and prep material for the GED. One local school district had obtained this grant, and the prep course was periodically offered at this school. Because of the grant, GED seekers were not required to pay for the course. But nobody, or at least very few, knew about it. The course was offered a couple of times per year, with only two or three people attending.

We had a need. And we had identified the resources. Our job was to figure out how to connect them. After conversation and a few meetings, the local community college agreed to host both the prep class and the GED test itself and allow the group who had obtained the grant funding to teach the prep class at the college. The need and resources were connected. Within a few short months, instead of two or three people attending the prep class, 20 or 30 were attending. Acts 4 Others did nothing more than ask some questions, facilitate conversations, and find the connecting point. As a result, individuals without a high school degree had a better, more accessible option to obtain their GED, eliminate the root cause of their poverty, and improve their situations.

In 2014, Acts 4 Others' focus shifted to homelessness. In the primary county where Acts 4 Others operates, the homelessness problem usually does not look like it does in more urban settings, with individuals sleeping on street corners or park benches. Instead, Acts 4 Others became aware of many individuals and families moving from friend's home to a friend's home. Or, they lived a night or two in their cars, then perhaps with a friend for a couple of nights. At times, a church would pay for a night or two in a hotel. This situation may not be as visible as individuals sleeping on street corners or park benches, but the struggle for these individuals and families to find and maintain affordable housing is every bit as real.

Churches and other local charitable organizations helped as much as possible, but such help is typically temporary, covering expenses for a day or two. Acts 4 Others stepped in to develop resources to facilitate a longer-term solution and provide the type of help to allow these individuals and families to sustain themselves without assistance.

The organization developed a process implemented over several months. It starts with an application submitted by potential participants. Next is a face to face meeting with the applicants. This meeting explores the applicant's background to understand why and how these individuals find themselves in their current situation. Sometimes this is the result of past, bad decisions. Sometimes this is because of circumstances beyond their control. Regardless, an applicant will not be disqualified based on his or her past. Instead, the past is an important piece of the puzzle to determine how to create a bridge to a better future. The other piece of the puzzle is what the applicant wants his or her future to be. During this initial meeting, they are asked to dream and share what they hope to achieve with a little help. Acts 4 Others' role is to facilitate the resources necessary to put those puzzle pieces together.

By understanding the applicant's past and desired future, a specific plan can be created, tailored to their unique circumstances, to provide resources to help the applicant remove whatever obstacles may be preventing the achievement of those dreams. The plan usually involves financial assistance for some period, often as long as six months, to help cover rent or other basic living expenses. This assistance frees the participants to focus on removing other obstacles, looking for a job, and developing the skills necessary to sustain employment. Each situation is different, and in exchange for the financial assistance, the participants agree to use the other resources identified by Acts 4 Others as necessary to remove the obstacles preventing their dreams from being achieved. Sometimes the plan includes emotional counseling. Sometimes financial counseling is required. The plan may include drug or alcohol rehabilitation and counseling. Educational support, such as connecting the participant with the GED program described above or facilitating some job-specific training or certification, is often included. Typically, the specific plan tailored uniquely to each participant includes several of these examples. Acts 4 Others partners with local churches and other charitable organizations to provide the resources to meet these needs.

Beyond the plan itself, relationship and support are vital to each participant's success. Acts 4 Others assigns a point person to each participant. Each point person is a volunteer. Their role is, quite simply, to be in relationship with the participants. This requires intentionality. The point persons check in regularly with the participants to help identify needs. They help hold the participants accountable. They connect them with resources. But mostly, they offer love and support. They pursue a relationship. They make sure the participants know someone believes in them and is present to help them achieve their dreams. While the participants' involvement with Acts for Others may end after a few months, their relationship with their point person often continues, no longer as a requirement but rather as a true friendship.

From 2014 to 2020, Acts 4 Others has connected approximately 200 family units to a better future by helping them avoid homelessness and develop long-term life skills and by offering lasting encouragement and relationships. This positive societal impact results from a small group of individuals choosing to look at the world around them, identify needs, and offer a solution. This is what intentionally loving hard looks like. And it is hard. It's hard because it requires time, effort, and commitment. It requires time away from other things.

And it's hard because success isn't guaranteed. Every Acts 4 Others participant has not had a successful result. One of the first participants we ever brought into the program ended with me testifying in court during an eviction proceeding. The relationship didn't work. Decisions by this participant required us to part ways with her and assist the landlord with an eviction. The program was brand new, and we did not have several years of success stories to offset this bad outcome. I questioned whether it was worth it. I wondered if we knew what we were doing and whether we could truly help people. But we moved forward and, over time, found success after success. There are still occasional bad outcomes. We can't avoid them. Loving others is sometimes messy and sometimes doesn't end well. However, if we continue loving despite the difficulties and obstacles, positive and life-changing impact will begin to occur.

With the homelessness program well-established, in 2018, Acts 4 Others began looking for new ways to make a difference in our community. The Wise Gives event was born. Wise Gives is a partnership between Acts 4 Others and the local hospital system to give services and goods to those in need in our county. The event is open and free to anyone in the community who needs services such as haircuts, eye exams, flu immunizations, winter clothing, blankets, general health screening, legal aid services, lab work, and other general services. In the continuing spirit of connecting needs with resources, service providers bring their skills to Wise Gives and set up shop for a few hours on a Saturday. Those needing the services show up and receive. In 2018, Wise Gives helped more than 500 individuals. In 2019, that number more than doubled.

Acts 4 Others is based on a simple scripture contemplating a world where people take care of each other. In Chapter 4, the Book of Acts says, "All the believers were one in heart and mind. No one claimed that any of their possessions was their own, but they shared everything they had. With great power, the apostles continued to testify to the resurrection of the Lord Jesus. And God's grace was so powerfully at work in them all that there were no needy persons among them. For from time to time those who owned land or houses sold them, brought the money from the sales and put it at the apostles' feet, and it was distributed to anyone who had need" (Acts 4:32-35). Connecting resources with needs. Acts

4 Others does this by intentionally loving its community. This love has an impact. We cannot change society all at once. But we can change society one person or family at a time.

Malala Yousafzai grew up in Pakistan. Her father founded his own school. Malala saw her brothers and male classmates find work while she and her female counterparts were limited to working within their homes. "For my brothers, it was easy to think about the future," Malala said. "They can be anything they want. But for me, it was hard, and for that reason, I wanted to become educated and empower myself with knowledge." As Taliban influence grew, female education became prohibited.[21]

Having the courage to fight for her right to an education, Malala gave an interview to a BBC blogger. She said, "I wanted to speak up for my rights. And also I didn't want my future to be just sitting in a room and be imprisoned in my four walls and just cooking and giving birth to children. I didn't want to see my life in that way." After this interview, she began speaking more publicly during the next few years. In 2012, when she was 15, Malala was shot in the head by Taliban gunmen, targeted as she left school. Malala survived, but her battle to recover was long and difficult. Nine months later, Malala spoke to a youth assembly at the United Nations in New York, a much bigger audience than she had before the shooting. "One child, one teacher, one book, one pen can change the world," she proclaimed.

Malala's struggle to love hard was not easy. In fact, it was far more difficult than I have ever experienced or can even imagine. But by continuing to offer her love in the fight for females around the world to receive an education, her impact stretched to the halls of the United Nations.[22]

Start somewhere. Look around and see what your world needs. Then fill the need by loving hard. When you do, you cannot imagine how far-reaching your impact will be.

Chapter 8

IMPACT ON POLITICS

*Recognition of the validity of other
perspectives and empathy with other
experiences may be required, but the
positive impact is significant. Pushing
each other further apart will accomplish
nothing. Listening to and understanding
each other, seeking common ground,
and loving each other despite our
differences, on the other hand, can
accomplish progress and leave
a lasting positive impact.*

In May of 1856, United States Senator Charles Sumner spoke to the Senate about whether Kansas should be admitted to the nation as a slave or free state. Senator Sumner was staunchly anti-slavery, and during his speech, he verbally attacked a couple of pro-slavery Senators with comments about their personal lives, unrelated to the issue at hand.

Preston Brooks, a member of the House of Representatives from South Carolina, took offense to Senator Sumner's comments about the two Senators, one of whom was also from South Carolina and Mr. Brooks' friend. Three days after Senator Sumner's speech, Representative Brooks took a cane, entered the Senate chamber, and hit Senator Sumner in the head with the cane. Brooks struck Sumner repeatedly, to the point where Sumner needed medical attention. The Senate historical archives' description of the event comments how "[o]vernight, both men became heroes in their respective regions," while the nation, "suffering from the breakdown of reasoned discourse that this event symbolized, tumbled onward toward the catastrophe of civil war."[23]

Senator Sumner's caning may be one of the most violent attacks among elected officials in Congress, but it is not the only one. Two years after the Sumner incident, about 30 House of Representative members brawled on the House floor.[24] In 1838, Congressman William Graves, a Whig, shot and killed Congressman Jonathan Cilley, a Democrat, during a duel in Maryland after Cilley's comments on the House floor critical of a prominent Whig newspaper editor.[25] Much of this violence occurred during the decades leading up to the Civil War, but it has by no means been limited to the highly tense pre-Civil War era. Attacks among Congressmen occurred as early as 1798 when Representative Roger Griswold attacked Representative Matthew Lyon with a cane on the House floor because Griswold was upset the House had failed to remove Lyon for spitting tobacco juice at Griswold. This followed tension arising between the two relating to President Adams's diplomatic position toward France.[26] In more modern times, in 1985 Democratic Congressman Thomas Downey confronted Republican Congressman Robert Dornan on the House floor following an exchange of heated words that turned personal after the two men disagreed about Nicaragua's crisis.[27]

We often hear how divided we are as a nation, but these stories demonstrate how dividing politics has always been. Now, we have social media and 24-hour news stations, so we hear immediately about every dispute and disagreement. We have video evidence revealing every time one elected official verbally attacks or makes fun of another or publicly criticizes others' views or policies. We live in an age when presidents and leaders can put their every thought on social media.

We are divided as a nation because we cannot respect, embrace, empathize, or even engage with others who see the world differently or have different governmental and societal expectations. It's certainly easier not to. In the middle of a disagreement, it's hard to love the other side. But what might happen if we were to embrace the tension and our differences and engage with each other anyway? What if we loved others well despite our differences and worked with each other instead of against each other? How much impact and meaningful change could be accomplished?

Later, we will look at a few leaders who put their differences aside, found common ground, and made real and lasting progress to solve difficult problems. These examples, however, are the exception rather than the rule. Whether within the halls of Congress, in your neighbor's backyard, or around the family Thanksgiving table, politics is almost always divisive. It brings out the worst in us. When faced with opposing political views, we typically react in one of two ways. Sometimes we lash out, angrily defending our position and arguing strongly to convince others our views are correct. At other times, we retreat and attempt to avoid the conversation altogether, quickly changing the topic. I am usually guilty of the latter. Neither is the best approach. And regardless of which of these two responses we lean toward, almost all of us form judgments and negative opinions about the person with the opposing views.

What if instead of aggressively engaging with or retreating from the person with whom we disagree, we engaged in political discussions with intentional love and empathy? What if we sought first to understand their perspective? What if we actually *listened*? What if we recognized their views and positions are formed largely out of their experience and perspective, which may be significantly different than our own? Instead of trying to convince others we are right or outrightly dismissing and avoiding others because we believe they are wrong, what if we assume the other person has good motives and attempt to engage with them in love and respect to find common ground?

Imagine that we were willing to put aside, at least temporarily, *some* of what we may like to achieve in exchange for listening and dialoguing to understand each other better and establish common objectives to move the ball forward. Politics and society are similar. Politics is simply the transformation and development of policies to address societal issues and problems. But when couched in a political context, tension levels escalate, and we find ourselves divided instead of unified to solve a problem. For example, not many people would disagree homelessness is a problem, and most people are open to finding ways, either personally or collectively as a society in the form of charitable-type assistance, to help homeless people. There are certainly exceptions, but most people are compassionate and would like to help. However, when the issue becomes political, presented in the context of a governmental solution to the problem and the use of public resources to address the issue, the unified desire to help homeless people quickly becomes polarizing. It's the same problem, but our reaction to the issue and willingness to work together to solve it looks quite different inside the political context than outside politics.

Patrick Kennedy authored and co-sponsored legislation intended to improve the mental health crisis by requiring insurance companies to offer mental health and addiction treatment similar to physical health benefits. Former Congressman Kennedy tells a fascinating story of how he finally succeeded in getting the bill passed and signed into law in 2008. He persuaded his father, Senator Ted Kennedy, to convince Senator Chris Dodd as chairman of the Senate Banking Committee, to add Representative Kennedy's mental health legislation to the bank bailout known as the Troubled Asset Relief Program during the middle of the 2008 financial crisis.[28] I recently heard Congressman Kennedy speak at a conference and describe how his mental health legislation became a reality. He discussed, without naming names, private conversations he had with members of the opposing political party during his efforts to gain support for the bill. He shared examples of how these other members of Congress privately supported the legislation because of personal encounters with mental illness in their own families. Publicly, however, they could not support the legislation because their political party opposed it. All recognized mental health as a significant societal problem and agreed we need to attack it. But as a political issue, it was polarizing.

For these reasons, politics and society deserved their own separate chapters in this book, and our loving-hard approach to each is quite different. As explored in the last chapter, to positively impact society, we need to look around us, see where there is a need, and get outside ourselves to do something about. It is best if we try to address those issues collaboratively, but we can also significantly impact them on our own. Politics, on the other hand, requires a more global and collective approach. In addition to identifying needs and problems and doing something about it, within the political context, we must also accept, respect, engage with, empathize with, and love hard people who have an entirely different perspective than us as to whether there's a problem in the first place and, if so, how best to solve it.

I started writing this book during the middle of the 2020 COVID-19 pandemic. Then, a couple of months later, while still writing the book, George Floyd, a black man, was killed by a white police officer in Minnesota, sparking Black Lives Matter protests across the country to promote awareness of, and hopefully solutions for, racial injustice. We might expect a pandemic and racial inequality to be societal issues everyone believes are a problem and works together on to seek a solution. Both issues, however, quickly became political and polarizing. Concerning the pandemic, we could have worked together to balance the need to prevent the spread of the virus and protect the health care system and most vulnerable members of the population with the equally pressing need to re-open the economy and get people back to work. Instead, we found ourselves as a nation in a political debate about whether the measures required to adequately respond to the virus were too inhibiting of our freedoms. Rather than embracing our differing perspectives to respond to all the problems created by the pandemic appropriately, it became a dividing, either/or type of issue. With respect to racial injustice in our nation, instead of listening to and learning from each other and seeking common ground, we entered a national debate about whether a problem even exists. Rather than recognizing that even though most law enforcement personnel are good people doing a difficult job, there may still be wrongs embedded in the culture that require a solution, we instead found ourselves arguing about the merits of protests and whether they were necessary. Some unnecessarily turned otherwise peaceful protests into violence and rioting.

We have seen video and images of groups standing

across from each other during these turbulent times, holding opposing signs and yelling at each other. Often, each group tries to be the loudest and drown out the other's message. We saw a group upset about measures intended to reduce the virus's spread angrily storm a state capital building. We have seen law enforcement desperately trying to keep Black Lives Matter protesters separated from counter-protestors. Occasionally, but far less often, we have seen images of individuals from opposing groups calmly talking to each other, seeking to understand and listen. I want so much more of the latter.

Loving hard requires more of us. We need to stop drawing lines in the sand and start stepping over the ones that already exist. We need to understand it is possible to have a conversation with others who disagree with us about difficult issues and pursue policies we believe in without attacking or judging those with opposing views. We need to be willing to listen to other perspectives and empathize with others' experiences. This is not easy. It requires us to stop. It requires us to listen. It requires us to educate ourselves. It requires us to assume that those with whom we strongly disagree also have good motives and want what they believe is best for our nation. Even if the conversations are hard and uncomfortable, we need to have them. Even when it's easier to walk away or angrily voice our position, we need to stop and listen and peacefully and respectfully engage. We need to be open to changing our minds or, at the very least, put our differences aside to find a path forward. Most importantly, after these hard conversations and listening to each other, we need to take action, together, to solve the problems.

People of faith seem to find this especially hard. We have a tendency to intermingle our politics and religion. As a result, we become even more entrenched in our political views and further convinced we are correct because we convince ourselves our faith requires the political position we are taking. We become less willing to listen and seek common ground because we somehow think doing so would make us untrue to our faith. In the case of Christianity, we shun those with opposing political views even going so far as to claim someone can't be a true Christian if they hold a certain view on a specific singular political issue.

One of the last things Jesus prayed for before his arrest and crucifixion was unity. According to John's record, Jesus said, "I am praying not only for these disciples but also for all who will ever believe in me through their message. I pray that they will all be one, just as you and I are one – as you are in me, Father, and I am in you. And may they be in us so that the world will believe you sent me. I have given them the glory you gave me, so they may be one as we are one. I am in them, and you are in me. May they experience such perfect unity that the world will know that you sent me and that you love them as much as you love me" (John 17:20-23). Jesus certainly did not mean his followers needed to agree on everything. In fact, the authors of these books record stories of the earliest Jesus followers disagreeing on a wide range of matters. Instead, Jesus wanted oneness and unity *despite* our differences. This was one of the last things on his mind before he died. He wanted it for us desperately. And we have messed it up so badly by using our differences to draw lines in the sand instead of embracing our differences and letting our faith unite us despite them.

We do the same thing in society as a whole, regardless of faith, letting our differences define and divide us. As a nation, we have so much in common. But those commonalities seem to matter less to us than our disputes and disagreements. We seek out those who are like-minded and ignore those who aren't. We let our fear of things and people we don't understand create anger and deception, instead of simply seeking ways to bridge the gap between our differing perspectives.

The reality is there are well-intentioned people on both sides of political issues. Let's be different and uncommon. As hard as it may be, let's love those with different political agendas and perspectives. Let's try to understand each other. Let's have uncomfortable and hard conversations with peace and love. How differently would our interactions with and perceptions of other people have been during the COVID-19 pandemic if we took this more uncommon approach? How differently would our interactions be with those who do not share our views about racial disparity and injustice?

During the recent events, Jenn and I have had hard conversations with our children, friends, and co-workers. Sometimes these people agree with us. Sometimes they don't. But we have tried during these conversations to emphasize the importance of loving others and valuing their perspectives and their experiences, no matter how different those may be from our own.

During the pandemic but before George Floyd's death and the following protests, we talked to our two teenage boys about the privileges and opportunities they have had, which others have not had. We talked about how those privileges and opportunities do not guarantee success or achievement and how hard work, commitment, discipline, and diligence are important but emphasized how the privileges and opportunities exist because of their race and socioeconomic status. There were questions, and even some disagreement.

A few days later, Mr. Floyd died, and the protests began. During the first few days of the protests, both of our boys had an experience relevant to our recent conversation which, in light of the events surrounding Mr. Floyd's death, brought clarity to their own privileges and opportunities and the need to empathize with others and attempt to understand others' perspective. My wife described their experience on social media as follows:

> Last week, Sam, Isaac, and about ten of their friends were in the 11 p.m. Whataburger line when the police pulled them out and asked some of them to get out of their cars. While waiting for Whataburger breakfast time to open, the boys had stopped at our church to play football in the parking lot, and someone called the police, thinking they were burglarizing the church. The police "detained" the boys and asked them questions but were polite and joked around with the boys, and once they confirmed that the church had not been burglarized, the boys were released. It was a minor inconvenience for our boys – they lost their spot in the long Whataburger line – and they had a funny story to tell their friends about the time they got "detained and questioned" by the police.
>
> Unlike moms of black and brown children, I have never had to discuss with my boys how to act when pulled over by the police or warn them that their skin color may cause anyone to act differently towards them. And I am painfully aware that the very incident involving my boys could play out differently for kids with black or brown skin – George Floyd was being detained over an alleged $20 forgery. My boys are very much aware of their white privilege, as well. In fact, while they were being "detained," Isaac and his friend, Mack, talked about the fact that their black

and brown friends may not have had the same treatment as them. This is unacceptable, and it must change.

I try to keep Facebook a happy place for me to look at pictures and catch up with friends and family. I have assumed that people who know me will know my heart and know what I believe and that my actions toward others will speak for themselves. But I am starting to read, and listen, and learn, and I now know that not being racist is not enough. We must actively be anti-racist. I do not know what that looks like or what actions I need to take yet, but I will continue reading, listening, and learning. I will continue to have conversations with my kids and friends, and family. I will correct wrongs to the best of my ability. And I will vote.[29]

So much impact and progress could be achieved if we would take an uncomfortable and uncommon loving-hard approach to politics and admit our own perspective and experience are not universal. While the examples of assaults and conflict in politics discussed at the beginning of this chapter appear to be the norm, there are also examples throughout history of the possible change we can achieve when we are intentional about working together and engaging with each other despite our differences. The first example comes from the very beginning of the nation. According to the Bipartisan Policy Center, in 1787, delegates to the Constitutional Convention were so divided over the question of congressional representation the Convention itself almost ended without a new Constitution. Roger Sherman of Connecticut presented a solution to appease both those who wanted proportional representation and those who wanted equal representation. His solution, a proportionally represented House and an equally represented Senate saved the day and is now entrenched in our Constitution. His solution had a lasting and positive impact. But as the Bipartisan Policy Center reports, although the idea "seems familiar to us now, [it] was so radical in 1787 that, at first, it was dismissed by the group. Eventually, the Connecticut Compromise – known now as the Great Compromise – was adopted, and the opposing sides in the debate each felt vindicated."[30]

The Bipartisan Policy Center offers several other examples of great impact achieved by people willing to embrace their differences and work together. For example, in 1860, President Lincoln put together a "Team of Rivals" when he appointed four of his fiercest political rivals to his cabinet because, as Lincoln explained, "he felt he had no right to deprive the country of its strongest minds simply because they sometimes disagreed with him."[31] Other examples include Senator Arthur Vandenberg's bipartisan foreign policy work with President Roosevelt in 1945 during post-war planning, which bridged a political divide on the question of how to treat a post-war Germany and Japan; the leadership of Democratic Senator Mike Mansfield and Republican Senator Everett Dirksen in 1964 to work together to gather enough support to end a filibuster of the Civil Rights Act and extend new rights to the nation's African Americans; and the joint effort of both political parties to work with President Eisenhower to create NASA and begin the work of putting a man on the moon. Joint, bipartisan efforts during which elected officials worked through their differences to find common ground also resulted in the Great Society legislation of 1965, the Endangered Species Act of 1973, the 1977 food stamp program, social security reform in 1983, tax reform in 1986, the Americans with Disabilities Act of 1990, welfare reform in 1996, the Children's Health Insurance Program of 1997, campaign finance reform in 2002, and the JOBS Act of 2012.[32]

All these examples, the result of joint and collaborative efforts by people with deep differing perspectives and agendas, have positively impacted millions of lives for decades. They show us how difficult issues do not have to be either/or situations and, instead, how we can positively impact millions of people and reflect the joined views of people who began the conversation in conflict and opposition. Recognition of other perspectives' validity and empathy with other experiences may be required, but the positive impact is significant. Pushing each other further apart will accomplish nothing. Listening to and understanding each other, seeking common ground, and loving each other despite our differences, on the other hand, can accomplish progress and leave a lasting positive impact.

Brené Brown has commented, "Empathy has no script. There is no right way or wrong way to do it. It's simply listening, holding space, withholding judgment, emotionally connecting, and communicating that incredibly healing message of 'You're not alone.'"[33] Ms. Brown has captured better than I can the concept of loving hard. When it comes to political differences, loving hard requires empathy. As Ms. Brown says, there is no right or wrong way to do it. But we must do it. As hard as it is, we must do better. We must seek to understand each other. And then we must find ways to act together to solve the problems we face.

Chapter 9

IMPACT ON LEADERSHIP

*If the leader loves his or her
followers hard and values them, the
potential impact of both the leader
and those being led is limitless.
But it's hard, and it requires a
generous spirit and a willingness to
put aside the leader's desires and
interests for the benefit of others.*

Leadership guru John Maxwell has said, "Leadership is influence. Nothing more, nothing less."[34] Leadership doesn't come from title or position. It comes from our ability to influence those around us. The question is, where are we leading people? How are we influencing them? Are we leading and influencing them positively or negatively? The answer lies in whether we make it about ourselves as the leader or the people we lead. As a leader, how much I care about the people I am leading and how much I seek to add value to them instead of me directly correlates to how well I am leading them and how much impact my leadership has on them. Loving hard in leadership requires us to value those we are leading more than ourselves and add value to their lives rather than our own.

I've had many opportunities to lead during my lifetime, and quite honestly, I wasn't very good at it during many of those years. My influence and impact, therefore, were more limited than they could have been. In high school, I was a class officer. Class officers did little during the high school years, at least in my experience. Mostly, being a class officer provided a good bullet point on college applications and early resumes. We had a role in planning prom and maybe a few other events. As I learned years later, and much to my dismay, the role also came with an expectation we officers would plan class reunions. The frequency and quality of those reunions have declined significantly since the 10-year reunion, and if my classmates had a chance to cast those high school votes again, I'm certain they would cast them differently. I wouldn't blame them.

While most aspects of being a class officer were insignificant, I recall one situation that carried a little more significance, at least at the time. Most of the graduating classes before ours held their graduation ceremony in the high school gym. Our class, the largest at that time, was too large for the gym. Different solutions were discussed. One involved staying in the gym but issuing a limited number of tickets to each student. One involved traveling to nearby communities to use a larger facility. One contemplated holding graduation at the high school football stadium, allowing an unlimited number of spectators, but the weather was potentially a factor.

Years of hindsight reveal this decision wasn't overly significant in the overall course of our lives. But at the time, it was something new and unprecedented, and there were differing and strong opinions on which option was best. I honestly don't remember which option I preferred. However, I do remember believing strongly, too strongly, that my preference was the best one. A meeting was scheduled with the entire class to discuss the issue and get input. The class officers led the meeting. Whatever my preference was, it had formed and solidified well before this meeting. I thought I knew what was best. I participated in the meeting, but I wasn't truly interested in what others had to say or their perspectives and preferences. At one point during the meeting, after a fellow student voiced a preference different than mine, I remember whispering to one of the other officers sitting next to me my perspective that we were wasting our time, and the rest of the class had elected us to make this decision for them.

If someone were teaching a class on how to be a terrible leader, they could start with me and this story. I understood nothing about how to lead. I thought my title "class officer" gave me the right to decide what was best for others, without any input or consideration of their perspective. During the next couple of decades, however, and despite my total failure of leadership as a teenager, life continued to present me opportunities to lead, and more importantly, to learn how to lead. I have served in church leadership. I have been elected to city leadership positions. I have been appointed to various civic boards and committees. I have led charitable and service organizations. I have led small groups of people and large groups. And I am now leading a hospital system.

Each of these has provided opportunities to learn how to be a better leader. The best leaders never fully arrive. They recognize leadership is a lifelong journey, requiring constant growth and development. I am still learning and developing as a leader. Too often, I don't get it right. I sometimes fail to lead well. But I have become a better leader over the years mainly because I now understand leadership is not about me. It's not about my title. It's not about my position. It's not about the authority I have over others. It's not about the level of my education or intelligence.

For too many years, I thought leadership came naturally, and one was either a born leader or not. Either you have it or you don't. I now understand leadership requires effort. It requires growth and seeking wisdom from mentors. Good leaders are lifelong learners, constantly educating themselves and learning from others. Leadership, at its core, is about adding value to others. I'm a slow learner. It took too long for me to shift my focus as a leader away from me and my abilities to, instead, how I can use my abilities and opportunities to help others grow and develop, discover their own gifts and talents, and understand their value to the world and how they can positively impact it.

Leaders who don't understand this are taking the easy approach to leadership. It's easy to make decisions when the objective is what's best for the leader. There is no need to consider how value is added to others. There is no need to involve others in the process or listen to them. Collaboration and engagement with others aren't necessary. There is no need to cast vision or explain the why behind decisions or actions. Involvement, collaboration, listening, and sharing vision and purpose are hard. They require effort and intentionality. Leaders who fail to recognize their number one purpose is to grow, develop, and add value to others, and who believe others should follow them simply because of the leader's position or authority, have it easy. Good leadership, on the other hand, is hard and starts with choosing to love others hard and put their interests above your own.

Even though I have learned how to be a better leader, the learning process never ends, and being a good leader requires me to set aside my natural tendencies intentionally. For example, I still tend to bristle when those I'm leading question my decisions. It irritates me. This is my natural reaction, even though I know it's wrong when I'm not intentional about welcoming the questioning and even criticism. Good leaders are adaptable. They are willing to admit when they are wrong. They are willing to revisit decisions when others present valid questions and flaws. My decisions are better when they are questioned. More questioning, input, and collaboration cause me to gather more information, leading to better decisions. Now, when questions and criticism come, I am learning to intentionally pause and consider how they will lead to better decisions and outcomes and avoid the natural irritation that would otherwise come. Good leaders must be willing to accept questioning and criticism and reconsider decisions already made if such questioning and criticism bring new information and factors to light.

Consider leaders you have had during your life. They may have been coaches, mentors, teachers, or bosses. How well did they lead? How willing were you to follow them? Did they expect you to follow them because of their authority over you? Or did you choose to follow them because they knew how to lead and did it well? Far too many leaders expect the former. Far too few lead well because they fail to understand leadership is, first and foremost, about valuing the people you are leading.

I have followed good leaders and bad leaders. I followed the bad leaders because I had to. I followed the good leaders because I wanted to. I remember one leader in particular who understood the importance of adding value to those you are leading. My first law firm job was with a large, multi-national law firm in Washington, D.C. Like many law firms, the firm primarily hired new lawyers from its summer associate program. Second-year law students were hired as summer associates. During the summer between second-year and third-year, those students worked at the firm for six to eight weeks, providing students the opportunity to learn about the firm and the firm to undertake a summer-long interview. Offers for permanent associate positions to begin the following year after the third year of law school were made at the end of this summer program, depending on how well they performed.

Each summer, the firm hired approximately 50 summer associates. There were approximately 500 lawyers in the Washington office alone and hundreds more in the other firm offices scattered around the globe. The firm's leader was a senior partner named Jim. His title was managing partner. When my group showed up for work on our summer program's first day, Jim greeted us. He knew all of our names. He knew which law school we attended. He was not involved in our interviews, so this was the first time he had met us. Yet he had taken time to study us and learn about us before we arrived. This wasn't even our first day of a permanent job, but of a summer job to allow the firm to see if we were good enough to earn a permanent offer. Despite the responsibilities of managing a multi-national business and overseeing hundreds of lawyers around the world, Jim had taken the time and been intentional about learning the names and backgrounds of approximately fifty students who were possibly going to spend only six to eight weeks with Jim's firm.

Jim's intentionality left a lasting impression on me. I didn't understand it at the time, but I now know this is what made Jim a strong leader. He valued those he was leading. What he did to learn our names and schools and background before ever meeting us may seem simple. But as a law student searching for a job and trying to find my place in the profession, I felt valued. And because Jim's seemingly simple act made me feel valued, I knew Jim was someone I could follow.

As an alumnus and fan of the University of Texas, I admire Mack Brown, the Longhorns football team's long-time coach, and have observed his strong leadership abilities. Like Jim at my first law firm, Coach Brown's successful leadership style begins with his love for his players and assistant coaches and his desire to see them succeed and add value to their lives. In the locker room in 2006, immediately after his team beat the University of Southern California for the national championship, Coach Brown's post-game speech reflected a leadership style based on a desire to add value to those around him. He recalled his speech as follows: "Then I said, 'Don't get in trouble. Don't spoil this wonderful moment in your life with something bad. And finally, I said, don't let this be the best thing that ever happens in your life. It's the best thing you can do in sports for this year. We can only win the national championship and be the best team and you've done that. So congratulations. But take this as an opportunity to be a better father and a better husband and a better person in the community.' The guys just looked at me like I was crazy when I said that, but 12 years later, when we see each other, they all show me pictures of their wives and kids, and they say, 'I finally understand what you were talking about in the locker room after the game.'"[35]

Describing his role as the leader of young men, Coach Brown said, "[E]very single year, no matter our record or what happened in the last game of the season, another one of my goals was always to have players leave my program better prepared for life than they were when they came in. Having had some hand in a player's success and happiness, now that I'm willing to call one of the best things that have happened in my life."[36] Coach Brown understands a leader's responsibility involves much more than merely expecting people to follow you because of a position of authority with the goal to achieve certain results for your team or business. Rather, he recognizes there are significant and impactful implications beyond the team or sport or business itself. By loving hard those being led and adding value to their lives, leaders like Coach Brown are equipping individuals to live their own lives of meaningful and positive impact. In 2019, after several years in the sports media while in coaching retirement, Coach Brown returned to the University of North Carolina, where he had coached before coming to Texas in the late 90s. He returned to coaching because he missed the players and missed the opportunity to lead them to something better. "The bond with these guys, seeing them get better, is just invaluable. And very few people get to do that in their lives," he said. "That's why coaches have trouble getting out of coaching. It's hard to win, and you have to win to stay, but if you can win and you get to stay, you can't measure the value of helping guys grow."[37]

Pay close attention to what he's saying here because it's really important. His objective isn't to lead people toward winning football games. His objective is to win football games to extend his opportunity to continue leading people to become better versions of themselves. This is what good leadership looks like – making a positive impact on those we lead can, in turn, prepare them to change the world around them.

This type of leadership doesn't simply happen. It doesn't come naturally. It requires intent. It requires development. It requires constant growth and learning by the one leading. It demands the leader to love those being led enough to have difficult conversations with them, to be present and transparent and authentic with them, all to develop the trust necessary for them to follow out of desire rather than position. The leader is obligated to over-communicate and explain why expectations are what they are and why things are done a certain way. It requires the leader to collaborate, listen, ask questions, and be open to being wrong. Michael Hyatt, a leader of leaders, has said, "I used to think leadership was about having the right answers, but now I understand it's about asking the right questions."[38]

The best way to become a better leader is to spend time with good leaders. Ask them questions. Listen to them. Watch how they love and lead those around them. Several months ago, one such leader entered my life. Since I entered the healthcare industry full time almost a decade ago, I've discovered this industry has a lot of really good leaders, mainly because people in health care take seriously their obligation to mentor, add value to, and share wisdom with others. Even in an industry full of strong leaders, Jim (not the one who led the law firm I once worked for) stands out. Jim is the CEO of a large, multi-hospital system in a large metropolitan area. The hospital system I lead is small by comparison. Yet, several months ago, Jim asked for time on my calendar and drove about an hour to my office to meet me. This is part of what Jim does and who he is. He is intentional about spending time with other leaders, partly to network within the industry but largely to develop relationships and find opportunities to mentor.

Jim and I have only known each other a few months, but I've learned much from Jim in a short amount of time about how to lead better. It is not just how to be a better hospital leader but also how to be a better leader of people in general. Jim and I first met shortly before the 2020 coronavirus pandemic began, and it could not have come at a better time. As I faced difficult decision after difficult decision, Jim provided much needed and appreciated guidance. He faced many of the same decisions within his organization. But he has a way of simplifying each problem and re-casting it with a unique perspective. However, the foundation of all of Jim's wisdom and guidance is his love for the people he is leading and his desire to see them succeed and live lives of impact.

Jim has shared many thoughts about how to lead in a difficult industry, but one piece of guidance stands out. During the pandemic, Jim shared the importance of being surrounded by good people with diverse backgrounds and perspectives and expertise and relying on those people to provide all the information needed to make good decisions. Jim explained how a good leader recognizes he or she lacks all the perspective, qualifications, background, or experience to make the best decision possible and the importance of asking others as many questions as necessary to obtain all the required information. In the middle of a pandemic, the timing of Jim's guidance was perfect, and I cannot overstate my appreciation for strong leaders like Jim who are willing to intentionally grow and add value to other leaders like me, even while dealing with their own difficult decisions and circumstances.

Jim's advice reminds me of Doris Kearns Goodwin's guiding words about leadership. Ms. Goodwin is an American biographer and historian who has written extensively about past American leaders. Ms. Goodwin advises, "Good leadership requires you to surround yourself with people of diverse perspectives who can disagree with you without fear of retaliation."[39]

A leader's willingness to do what Ms. Goodwin suggests reveals the most important characteristic good leaders share. Humility. Many misunderstand humility to mean thinking less of oneself. But it's not. Instead, humility means to think of yourself less and others more. It requires the leader to understand others' value and their unique perspectives, and the resulting unique positive impact they can have if you as their leader listen to them and create an opportunity for them to thrive and grow. If the leader loves his or her followers hard and values them, the potential impact of both the leader and those being led is limitless. But it's hard, and it requires a generous spirit and a willingness to put aside the leader's desires and interests for the benefit of others.

Mary Parker Follett was an American social worker, management consultant, philosopher, and pioneer in the field of organizational behavior in the late 1800s and early 1900s. She has been called the "Mother of Modern Management." Her ideas were based on the simple concept that a leader should empower and value those being led. Her most famous quote captures the essence of her leadership beliefs, as she said, "Leadership is not defined by the exercise of power but by the capacity to increase the sense of power among those led. The most essential work of a leader is to create more leaders."[40]

As much as I try, I often fail to apply this as I lead people and organizations. Sometimes I make it about me and my plans and ideas. I hope, though, I am learning to admit my mistake when this happens, to understand the unsettled feeling left behind when I fail to value and add value to those I'm leading, and to have the hard conversation to fix it. Recently, during a team meeting with my vice presidents and senior leaders, one of the vice presidents shared his concerns about our organization's new approach to establishing and improving culture and focus on becoming a more excellent organization. This vice president desires and seeks excellence as much as all of us, but he was having trouble understanding the practical aspects of our new ideas and approach. He voiced those concerns, as he should. I misunderstood his perspective. Rather than listening to him and valuing him and collaborating with him to resolve his questions, I snapped at him. My words in response to his valid questions left him the impression his perspective didn't matter.

My response demonstrated poor leadership. I felt his perspective was critical of the new direction, and I took it personally. Rather than leading, I reacted. But the conversation left me feeling unsettled. Several days later, I approached him, and we talked about it. This time, I listened, and by listening, I better understood his perspective. I understood he had no intent to be critical. He simply wanted to understand the new direction better to lead his people well in the same direction I was leading the organization. As badly as I failed when he first raised his questions, I hope my willingness to revisit it and admit my shortcomings showed good leadership.

Becoming a better leader is a lifelong process. I will not stop learning. But I have learned that for me to be the best possible leader I can be, I must love those I'm leading no matter how difficult or whether I benefit in any way. I must value them and seek ways to help them grow and develop their unique gifts and talents, and perspectives. When I do, my impact as a leader is far greater.

Chapter 10

IMPACT ON RELATIONSHIPS

*Our approach to all relationships,
whether it's one we find easy or one we
find difficult, should be to offer the type
of unlimited goodwill and benevolence
we'd like them to offer to us, regardless
of whether they actually do. It's a type
of love that is absolutely unreasonable
by our typical standards but will have
the most significant impact on our
relationships and the world around us.*

P erhaps a chapter on relationships should have been where
the book started because the reality is how and whether
we love hard, and its impact on all of the life components
addressed in this book begins and ends with how we relate to
each other. If we take this chapter's concepts concerning our
interpersonal interactions and relationships and apply them
to faith, politics, society, leadership, family, and all other

aspects of our lives, our potential for positive impact on each other and on each of those life components could be fulfilled.

We interact with other people every day. How much do we engage in these relationships? Are we intentional about our engagement? How are we impacting these people? Positively or negatively? When tension or relationship difficulty arises, do we press in and engage further, or do we back away and choose comfort instead? Do we perceive our interpersonal relationships as benefitting ourselves or those with whom we are interacting? Our answers to these questions drive how successful we can be in loving hard whoever we are interacting with at any given time.

You have likely noticed a trend in previous chapters revealing how so much of what I have learned in relating to others and loving them hard results from too frequently failing to do what I should. There are too many examples to share when it comes to my shortcomings in applying the "love hard" principles to my own interpersonal relationships. But I'll provide at least one.

It's important to understand as we are examining relationships, we cannot simply look only at those close relationships in our lives. Although perhaps not hard enough, we naturally work harder at loving those who are regularly in our lives, either at home or work or our other frequent interactions. Our relationships, however, also include those with whom we may interact infrequently or even only once. We encounter these types of relationships every day. We need to examine how we interact during these relationship encounters with strangers to determine how well we intentionally love others and our true impact.

Our children have played a lot of basketball games over the years. I cannot count the number of games I've attended. Sometimes I have coached their teams. My preference is to simply be a parent in the stands, which has happened more as they have gotten older. I'm competitive, and sometimes my competitive spirit leads me to interactions with referees I quickly regret. I know it's only a game. I know the outcome of a youth sports game has no bearing on life in general. Over the years, I believe I have drastically improved in these interactions and hope my family agrees. Staying preoccupied helps, which is why I now use an app on my phone to keep stats. I've found I'm far less likely to engage with the game's participants if I'm busy trying to enter points, rebounds, assists, and steals. But since our oldest started playing at a young age, at times, my competitive juices have overcome my good sense and caused me to fail miserably during a few personal interactions.

One stands out. When Isaac was in third or fourth grade (yes, I recognize how young that is and how meaningless this particular game truly was), I took issue with a referee's refusal to call the other team's repeated violation of a rule. I am certain the referee had the good sense to recognize, more so than me, the participants' young age and the need to let them develop, so he exercised some discretion in enforcing the game's rules. This logic failed me at the time. I have learned if you want the referee to hear you and know of your complaint, you should not vocalize your complaint while the action is happening or while the fans are cheering or yelling. If so, your complaint will be lost in the noise. Instead, it's best to wait until things are quiet. Then you can be certain the referee will hear you. I timed it just right and voiced my concerns with his decision-making. He stopped, walked over to me, and engaged me in conversation. All eyes in the gym were on us. It was not my proudest moment, as confirmed by the look on Isaac's face as I caught his eyes, which revealed his thought, "I can't believe this is happening."

I don't know the referee's name. I likely haven't interacted with him since then and probably never will. But by adding negativity and a narrow-minded perspective to the situation, I no doubt negatively impacted him, others in attendance, and my son. Whether we are interacting with lifelong friends, family members, co-workers, casual acquaintances, or people we encounter only once, every interaction and every moment is an opportunity to impact our environment positively.

Relationships are hard. They require work and effort. They require us to love the other person even when it's not easy. *Especially* when it's not easy. They require extra effort when the person with whom we are in a relationship or interacting is difficult and disagreeable. They demand we care as much or more about the other person as ourselves. But the potential reward of our effort is significant. Sometimes an easy relationship with those closest to us may become difficult. And sometimes those we may consider "enemies" become close friends if we work at it and don't give up. Regardless, relationships require hard work, and they deserve our best efforts because of the possible impact when we love each other well. The potential positive impact is not limited to only the individuals directly in the relationship but may extend far beyond.

The relationship between John Adams and Thomas Jefferson, numbers 2 and 3 in the line of U.S. Presidents, provides a glimpse of the intentional effort relationships require and the positive impact that is possible when the parties give that effort. Adams and Jefferson met during the revolutionary years of the 1770s and 1780s when both were young men. Adams was only 40 when the Declaration of Independence was signed, and Jefferson was 33. They became close friends. They traveled overseas together to advance the new nation's causes. Their families became close. Their mutual goals and objectives created a deep bond between them.[41]

Beginning in the 1790s, after the war had been won and

the new nation began to form an identity, those mutual goals and objectives began to diverge. Politics happened. Political parties formed. Adams and Jefferson found themselves members of opposing political parties. Both served in George Washington's administration, Adams as vice president and Jefferson as Secretary of State. By the 1796 election, the fractures in their relationship were so deep and the divide between them so great that Jefferson resigned from the Cabinet and ran for president against Adams. Once close confidants and friends, they had become political enemies.[42]

Adams won the presidency in 1796. In 1800, Jefferson beat Adams in a highly partisan and nasty campaign. Adams refused to attend Jefferson's inauguration. They did not speak or communicate with each other for over a decade. After their mutual friend Benjamin Rush intervened and pushed for reconciliation, they finally started communicating with each other again in 1812. They wrote back and forth during the next 14 years until they died on the same day, July 4, 1826, the Declaration of Independence's 50th anniversary.[43] During their last years, those final letters reveal a return of affection for each other and left the world with historical details we otherwise would have lost without their reconciliation.

To love each other well and have the best possible relationships, we must be willing to be uncomfortable. Adams and Jefferson had spent years as political enemies. Their actions and words left wounds. It would have been simpler and more comfortable for each of them to spend their later years in other pursuits rather than rebuilding a broken relationship. They had already walked away from each other. Why choose the difficult and uncomfortable path leading to reconciliation?

The relationship between these two men required hard work. It required forgiveness. It involved both intentionally setting aside their personal feelings of anger and resentment and listening to a mutual friend's wisdom and guidance. In the end, they chose to love each other, no matter how hard it was and despite years of tension, difficulties, and circumstances which drove them apart. They recognized the impact of their mutual, intentional decision to love each other and reconcile. Their restoration and reconciliation positively impacted them and their families, bringing joy and reviving fond memories during their last few years. More importantly, their restored relationship had an impact on generations of Americans who followed, providing important pieces of history and hope to a new, evolving nation.

We should embrace the lack of comfort in our relationships instead of running from it. We should run toward the tension and unresolved questions. We should welcome those relationships that challenge and stretch us. We should fully engage in the hard conversations with those who see the world so differently from us because in the middle of this engagement, we can discover understanding.

No doubt, the more comfortable path is simpler. But most of us, myself included, are far too quick to choose it. We avoid difficult situations and conversations. We walk away from others when we feel wronged. And we create justifications for these decisions when we simply don't like to be uncomfortable when relationships become difficult.

But the times we grow the most, as individuals and in our relationships, are the times we are willing to be uncomfortable. This occurs when we embrace the tension. Or when we listen and try to understand someone whose perspective is entirely different than ours. We are impacted most when we are open to what we can learn from others who may be difficult and may be wrong, but who nevertheless have something to offer. Rather than simply writing them off and walking away, we should recognize the personal growth we can experience or the positive impact we can have on the other person.

When we enter the conversation with an openness to being challenged and stretched, we often experience both.

I have those people in my life, and hopefully, you do in yours also. These are the people we may frequently disagree with, but we engage anyway and allow ourselves and our beliefs to be questioned. Sometimes my views change because of these relationships. Sometimes my views solidify and strengthen. I need to be open to either possibility. Instead of judging or rejecting others because of our differences, let's be open to moving toward and learning from each other and continuing to engage with each other even if our differences never get resolved.

Far too often during my life, I've chosen the easier and more comfortable path in my relationships. I've wanted too strongly to be right, so I haven't allowed others to question or challenge me. I've let the desire to "stand up for what I believe in" cause me to push others away. I've chosen to walk away from relationships when they become too difficult, often with the attitude of "life's too short," failing to understand the impact which is possible if I'd simply decided to love the other person more than my own comfort and satisfaction.

Everyone we encounter deserves for us to make a better choice. They deserve our hard love, no matter how difficult they may seem. Does anybody come to your mind right now? Maybe a specific person. Or maybe a group of people. Perhaps members of the opposing political party. Or another church, group, organization, or nation. If so, run toward them. Engage with them. Commit to the relationship. This doesn't mean you need to agree with them or join them or change your views. But be open to the dialogue and the conversation and the chance, as small as it may seem, that at least some of your firmly held beliefs may be wrong and these other, difficult people may teach you something.

And let's not overcomplicate things by justifying the

boundaries of our love. Maybe you think you can love others, but you don't have to like them. Or you will use "tough love," whatever that means. Or we can love them without truly helping them. We can come up with justification after justification for choosing something less than true, loving-hard engagement. Whether they be easy or difficult, our approach to all relationships should be to offer the type of unlimited goodwill and benevolence we'd like them to offer to us, regardless of whether they actually do. It's a type of love that is absolutely unreasonable by our typical standards but will have the most significant impact on our relationships and the world around us.

This type of love in our relationships and interactions with those we encounter is so important because it is both life- and world-changing. Consider the story of Adams and Jefferson. The hard love and intentionality between them - and their friend Benjamin Rush - restored their personal relationship, bringing peace and joy during their final years. The impact did not end there, however. Because of the restorative love between two individuals, generations of Americans have been affected by their story. Efforts between two old men during their later years show us it's possible to love each other despite our differences. It's possible to have restoration no matter how difficult the circumstances have become. It's possible to have respect, admiration, and fondness for each other even when our views and perspectives may be adverse. And it's possible to hope for more, for something better, regardless of how bad things may seem in the moment. Loving those we want to love is easy. Loving those we would rather not love, whether lifelong enemies or former friends or family members with whom we now have conflict and tension, is hard. But the results of this kind of love are far-reaching and lasting.

Leanne Friesen, a Canadian pastor, visited Lebanon

during the height of the Syrian civil war and refugee crisis. A long history of conflict exists between the Lebanese and Syrian people, going back well before the recent Syrian civil war. They have a shared history which has resulted in tension and hatred developed over decades. They consider each other enemies.[44]

During her visit to Lebanon, Ms. Friesen observed this fractured history. She heard a Lebanese pastor tell the story of his father being killed by Syrians. She heard a Lebanese woman describe standing at gunpoint before Syrian soldiers while holding her infant in her arms. Another Lebanese church leader explained how his entire town had once been under siege by Syrians for 100 days with no food or medical supplies. She heard story after story of pain, loss, grief, and hatred between these two nations.[45]

But Ms. Friesen also saw the positive impact of enemies intentionally loving each other despite their history of conflict as the Lebanese people suddenly found Syrian refugees flooding into Lebanon during the Syrian civil war. How difficult must it have been for the Lebanese people to choose to intentionally love a group of refugees from a nation long considered to be an enemy? Ms. Friesen described the life-altering love offered by many in Lebanon to their Syrian enemies who had now become neighbors. When they found themselves surrounded by their enemies, and those enemies were hungry, lonely, and homeless, many in Lebanon chose love over hate. The pastor whose father was killed now has a church reaching out to thousands of Syrian families. Ms. Friesen described how the Lebanese pastor invited a Syrian refugee to the front of the church and washed his feet to show the rest of the church how to love and forgive. His church has grown from 60 to 900 people, with most being Syrian refugees. The woman held at gunpoint with her infant is now part of a group caring for 500 displaced Syrian families.

Other Lebanese churches are providing food, job training, and education to Syrian refugees.[46]

Out of hatred and conflict has come love, hope, joy, and peace. Loving hard in the middle of our most difficult relationships can have this kind of impact if we would simply choose to do it. Our love for others despite what they may have done to us or - what they may do for us - may very well be what brings the restoration and revelation necessary to change lives and change the world. In his book, *Everybody Always: Becoming Love in a World Full of Setbacks and Difficult People*, Bob Goff wrote, "The way we treat people we disagree with the most is a report card on what we've learned about love."[47] Loving others in the middle of conflict and difficulties may be unexpected. It may be the opposite of what others would advise we do. It may be intimidating and uncomfortable. And it is certainly hard. But it's how our relationships reach their fullest potential and have the greatest impact.

Within a few hours of me writing what I thought would be the last paragraph of this chapter, I received a text from a friend. Jenn and this friend's wife serve together on our local school board. A recent issue the school board is attempting to address has created division and conflict between Jenn and his wife, and he raised his concerns in his text to me. I disagree with his position and perspective. I disagree with the conclusions he has reached about how Jenn has responded to the situation. Frankly, his text annoyed and frustrated me, and my natural inclination was to either retreat and walk away or lash out. Neither would have been the correct approach.

I don't think it's a coincidence his text arrived when it did. I cannot write and teach on these subjects without a willingness to put them into practice. What does loving hard require of me (and Jenn) in this situation? We need to be willing to be uncomfortable and have hard conversations with them. We need to run toward them even if they are running away from us right now. No matter how hard or contrary to my natural inclinations, loving hard requires this of me. Not to compromise my views or Jenn's views or agree when we don't. But to seek to understand and heal and restore *despite* our differences. Our relationship with them is worth it. And the potential positive impact on the four of us and perhaps others is significant if Jenn and I are willing to take these hard steps in love toward our friends. I hope if this friend and his wife ever read this book, they can confirm we loved them well in the middle of difficult circumstances. I'm certainly going to try.

Chapter 11

IMPACT ON JOY

Choosing to love others well in an intentionally and outwardly focused life, which both flows naturally from an internal joy and itself brings us a joy we could not otherwise have, allows us to spread joy, hope, encouragement, and peace within our circles of influence.

Whether we love hard deeply impacts our relationships and interactions with others, but it also has an impact on how we feel ourselves. We all want to experience joy. But most of us don't know what joy even means, and we certainly don't understand how to find it. We spend so much time pursuing joy, or more accurately happiness, in circumstances, relationships, wealth, and accumulation of stuff. We let our temporary emotions drive our behavior. What if, instead, we let our intentional, active love for others drive our behavior? How much joy would we experience by loving others hard and having an impact? When we do this well, our circumstances and difficulties matter less. Loving others well and having impact flows from an inner joy, but in an ironic circle, intentionally loving and serving others also feeds and grows our inner joy.

It's important to start with an understanding of what joy is and, more importantly, what it is not. We often use the terms happiness and joy as if they are interchangeable. They aren't. If you google "joy v. happiness," you will find several explanations of their differences. Mindvalley provides a good one, explaining how "joy and happiness are two distinct forms of pleasant emotional states" but "are *not* the same thing." [48] While happiness is "external and fleeting," dependent on "external things, situations, and experiences," and personal in nature, joy is "an *internal* affair that is *self-existent* and does not depend on external factors" and is "universal" and permanent.[49]

Happiness is based on our external situation and circumstances. Joy comes from something within. Mindvalley refers to it as the "universal fountain of joy." As C.S. Lewis said, "I sometimes wonder whether all pleasures are not substitutes for joy."[50] For many, this "universal fountain" is our faith. Some non-faith readers may be thinking about how Christians or other people of faith so often seem to be the least joyful people we encounter. I don't disagree. I've been there myself at times. But if we are truly living out our faith and have truly received God's gift to us, we cannot help but find the joy, hope, and peace it should bring. If you are not a person of faith, please keep reading. I've known very joyful people who did not consider themselves to be people of faith. They, too, had a joy coming from somewhere within that was not based on external circumstances, relationships, or possessions. I encourage all of you to look in, and not out, to find joy. "Where can I find my joy?" is one of the most important questions we must ask ourselves. Do we look for joy in our circumstances or possessions or relationships or other external factors over which we have very little true control? Or do we live with joy based on something within us which is outside our control and which provides hope and peace regardless of what's happening externally around us?

Our impact on this world depends largely on how we answer those questions. Once we learn how to find joy from our faith or those other internal "universal fountains of joy," we have taken a significant step toward leading an outwardly focused, loving-hard life. Those who look for joy in external things or circumstances cannot help but be self-centered and inwardly focused. They need to seek more and accumulate more in their quest for joy. These external needs drive their emotions and feelings. Finding the intrinsic joy described by Mindvalley and available to all of us, on the other hand, frees us to focus on others more than ourselves and to love others well and hard.

In the Declaration of Independence, we find these famous words, "We hold these truths to be self-evident, that all men are created equal, that they are endowed by their Creator with certain unalienable Rights, that among these are Life, Liberty and the pursuit of Happiness." I love this statement. It captures so much of our nation's potential and the values we are trying to achieve. But honestly, I often wish the authors hadn't included "pursuit of happiness" or at least had chosen a different phrase.

"Pursuit" indicates one must *do* something to obtain it or achieve it. I'm not sure exactly what Thomas Jefferson and the other authors meant, but we have turned the phrase "pursuit of happiness" into this concept of the "American Dream." We believe we should spend our lives pursuing and accumulating things, status, and wealth. We define success in those terms. In doing so, the "pursuit of happiness" and the "American Dream" become dangerous pastimes as they cause us to focus on ourselves instead of using our various gifts and talents to love others well and have a lasting impact.

I'm not aware if the authors of the Declaration of Independence ever attempted to explain what they meant by "pursuit of happiness." But others have. Emory University's religion and theology professor Brent Strawn in the *Emory News Center Report* has provided one of the best explanations, and he hints at the difference between happiness as we so often "pursue" it and happiness as a state of being which, in reality, is joy. Professor Strawn explains how most people think of "pursuit" as "chasing happiness," meaning to somehow seek or go after it. He further explains how much this understanding differs from what the founders meant, noting how at the time the Declaration was written, the "pursuit of happiness" meant "practicing happiness" rather than "chasing or seeking it." [51] According to Strawn, "*seeking* happiness is one thing, but actually *obtaining* it and *experiencing* it – *practicing* happiness! – is an entirely different matter," and because the "pursuit of happiness" is listed as an unalienable right along with "life" and "liberty," it is a "quality of existence."[52]

Perhaps any confusion could have been eliminated if our forefathers had chosen the phrase "state of joy" instead of "pursuit of happiness." If so, maybe instead of being in constant pursuit to accomplish, obtain, and accumulate more for ourselves, we'd find the internal contentment and peace which, according to Professor Strawn, Jefferson and his friends truly intended by the phrase they chose to include in the Declaration. What I like most about Professor Strawn's explanation is his profound conclusion that the true meaning of the Declaration's words should lead us away from our own happiness and toward "all citizens' happiness." In other words, it is not about me or what's best for me. It is about what's best for all of us, collectively.

When we start from a *state* of joy rather than a *pursuit* of happiness, we are best positioned to see what's best for others by loving them and having an impact. Joy requires first recognizing it's not about us, and we cannot control our circumstances. Instead, we are here for a purpose to live outwardly focused lives and have a lasting and meaningful impact on the people around us. How we carry out this purpose, given our unique abilities and talents, will look different for each of us. But we all have this similar purpose of loving others and having an impact. And, ironically, we end up being much more joyful ourselves when we choose to focus on others and love them hard instead of pursuing what's best for us.

I don't mean to imply it's easy to live in a state of joy with a focus on loving others rather than improving our own situations. I know life is hard and full of difficulties. We face challenges. For some of us, these challenges last longer than for others, sometimes lasting a lifetime. I do not want to minimize these difficulties. But this makes it even more important for those who find joy, through faith or otherwise, to spring from a foundation of inner joy to use their time and resources to help improve others' lives and love others well.

In the New Testament's Book of Philippians, often called the Book of Joy, Paul wrote about joy despite his own worldly circumstances, which found him frequently imprisoned, challenged, and persecuted. And most notably, his description of joy reveals the state of joy found in a life committed to loving and serving others. Despite constant challenges and struggles, Paul wrote and taught about always rejoicing despite our circumstances (Philippians 1:18-19), praying for others with joy (Philippians 1:4-5), receiving each other with joy (Philippians 2:29), and being unified with others (Philippians 2:2). In each of these descriptions, Paul connects our joy to how we love and relate to other people.

Reading through this list, I'm left wondering how often we truly do these things and how much more joyful our lives could be if we did. How often do we pray for others with joy, or are our prayers mostly about ourselves and whatever our current circumstances are? And if we pray for others, who do we pray for? Only those people we like and with whom we agree? Or do we also pray for those who think differently, look differently, or disagree with us? Do we do it with joy? Do we rejoice in the middle of our current hardships? It's difficult to see past our current circumstances, especially if those circumstances are bad. But the type of joy that comes from within and which can be found in loving and serving others supersedes whatever is happening in our lives right now. Do we receive each other with joy, welcoming and helping and encouraging those around us? Or do we only consider others when it's convenient for us and otherwise avoid or even become bothered or angry when we are inconvenienced? Do we live under a "me and mine" philosophy of life, or do we open our arms to our neighbors, *all* neighbors, even those with whom we disagree or do not understand? Do we hoard and accumulate for ourselves, or share and give generously and freely? With an outward perspective and focus, what happens to our level of generosity? Are we concerned primarily about having enough for retirement and meeting our own needs? Or, alternatively, if we love hard and search for impact with our finances, are we more fulfilled and content than if we had more money in the bank?

The last item in Paul's list speaks about the joy which comes from being unified with others. This may be the most interesting topic Paul writes about and the action in his list at which we are the worst at actually doing. So often, we fail to recognize that what outrages me may not outrage you.

And what outrages you may not outrage me. We are unified with those who are like us and agree with us but remain divided with everyone else. Instead of making so many assumptions about what others think and believe and letting our differences divide us, how much more joyful would we be if we instead focused on our connection points and those places where we can find unity with each other?

True joy is not based on our current circumstances, or what we do, or what we have, or what we don't have, or anything happening in the world right now. But this concept of the American Dream and the Pursuit of Happiness has become so warped and distorted it is the single largest detriment to our ability to experience the joy God intended for us. And in turn, it is a significant obstacle to our ability to impact the world to our best and fullest capability. We spend our time thinking we need some thing, or some one, or some place, or some experience, to make us happy. And we pursue these things, even as they come and go, developing resentment and outrage toward those we perceive have taken them from us or prevented us from getting what we believe we are entitled to or simply have something we don't. Others see this in us, and our impact becomes minimal, or negative, or both.

Alternatively, choosing to love others well in an intentionally and outwardly focused life, which both flows naturally from an internal joy and itself brings us a joy we could not otherwise have, allows us to spread joy, hope, encouragement, and peace within our circles of influence. How we treat and love each other and those who aren't like us, and how we take care of those who can't take care of themselves, and how we love our enemies when others say we should be hating and fighting them, all while experiencing our own difficult struggles and circumstances, both impacts our ability to be joyful and reveals whether we have an internal joy. These choices also directly correlate to the lasting impact our lives will have.

The things and circumstances of this world are often hard, and I don't mean to dismiss them easily. There are times to mourn. There are times to be sad. There are times to fight for important issues and causes, mainly when doing so will improve the lives of others. But we have a choice even in those difficult situations. We can react in anger and outrage and impatience with a lack of trust. Or we can react in peace and hope and joy, "rejoicing in all things." This will be observed by those around us and determine whether we affect the world in a way that spreads joy and draws people to us, or diminishes joy and pushes them away.

I wrote in earlier chapters about my career path. I spent many years pursuing happiness until I finally understood true joy could not be pursued. Now, with an underlying internal joy driving a desire to love and serve others and be more outwardly focused, my own joy grows far more than it did during my years of pursuit. Those closest to me will tell you I certainly still have more selfish moments and days than I'd care to admit. But I can more quickly return to joyfulness with a simple reminder that it's not about me and an intentional choice to shift my focus outward. This is our choice every single day. Will we live in the pursuit of happiness, trying to obtain happiness and pleasure from people and things and circumstances? Or, will we rejoice always, and as a result of this continuous joy, regardless of whether our current circumstances are good or bad, choose to love others well, spreading our joy and having the positive and lasting impact we are all capable of having on this world?

Chapter 12

BE NOT AFRAID

*Something must shift and make room
for it. Something new must lead us to
it. The fears which hold us back must
be replaced by love. We cannot be led by
fear and expect to have the positive and
lasting impact of which we are capable.*

W e've talked about how much positive impact we can
have by loving hard. So why don't we choose to do
so more often? It's difficult to love hard, and fear is the
primary obstacle. Fear of rejection. Fear of failure. Fear
of tension. Fear of difficulty. Fear of being uncomfortable.
Fear of things, people, and places we don't understand.
As discussed throughout this book, the best way to have a
positive and lasting impact in this world is to love others in
a way that is counterintuitive and difficult. But to do this, we
need to understand the fears holding us back and how we

can overcome these fears, which in turn allows us to love hard and change the world.

John Allen Chau was a 26-year-old American missionary from Washington state and a sports medicine graduate from Oral Roberts University when he visited North Sentinel Island in the middle of Bengal's Bay between India and Malaysia. North Sentinel Island is the home of one of the world's most remote and isolated tribes. They are entirely untouched by civilization. In November of 2018, John visited as a missionary to share his faith and his love for a group of people he had never met. When he attempted to reach the island, members of the tribe shot arrows at him with bows. He fled to his fishing boat.[53]

He went back a day or two later but was killed by the native tribe when he arrived. Many said he was crazy to return. Perhaps he was. India prohibited travel to the island, and the dangers were clear. But he knew exactly what he was doing and why he was going. He knew the dangers and chose, in the name of loving hard, to go anyway. He wrote to his parents before he left, "You guys might think I'm crazy in all this, but I think it's worth it to declare Jesus to these people. Please do not be angry at them or at God if I get killed."[54]

Sometimes we hear these types of stories but don't give them much thought because they seem so unreal and far-fetched. But Mr. Chau was a typical American college graduate who, despite very real and certain fears, chose to risk his life in the name of loving hard. I need to make it clear I'm not advocating loving hard requires taking the risks Mr. Chau took with his life and that his decision to try to convert the North Sentinel Island people was a good one or the correct one. In fact, I think it's fair to question the wisdom of his decision to try to convert a group of people voluntarily living in isolation and who have made their desire to be left alone very clear any time outsiders have tried to visit. Articles about his story and the aftermath of his death explain how many have questioned him and those who influenced his faith in a manner that drove him to this decision. Such criticism is fair. However, I don't think we can question Mr. Chau's motives, and I've included his story in this chapter not to endorse his actions and decisions but to demonstrate how love can overcome fear. It seems clear he believed strongly enough in sharing his faith to a group of people he did not know but chose to intentionally love hard, that any risk to himself was secondary to his love for them. How can we learn from people like Mr. Chau to love hard in the interest of positively impacting others *despite* our personal fears?

I can't speak to the fear-not topic without dipping into what is perhaps the fundamental foundational tenet of my Christian faith. As with other areas where I've discussed my faith in this book, however, I believe there are lessons here that are relevant to all readers, whether you consider yourself to be a person of faith. The story of humanity's fear and how it, too often, is the driving force behind our decisions and actions begins with the earliest recorded human stories. Whether allegorical or historical, the Genesis story of Adam and Eve teaches us about fear and its impact. According to the story, after Adam and Eve ate the apple despite God's instructions not to, they hid from God because they were afraid.[55] Their shame, because of their actions, caused them to fear God, whom they had disobeyed. Fear was the consequence of their poor decision.

It's important to note the difference between feeling afraid and being afraid. A feeling of fear is normal and is often the correct and healthy response to a situation. For example, if we are being attacked or we are threatened with harm, our feeling of fear causes us to react and hopefully protect ourselves. My family likes to go to the lake. One of our favorite lakes in Texas is called Possum Kingdom Lake. On this lake, there are a couple of islands in the form of rock formations protruding from the water. They are affectionately referred to as Hell's Gate, and they rise about 90 feet above the water. Cliff diving competitions are held there. I have hiked to the top of Hell's Gate, and while there, I was curious what it would be like to jump to the water. If the cliff diving competitors could do it, surely I could. This thought was fleeting, quickly replaced by the feeling of fear of the bodily harm certain to occur if I satisfied my curiosity. This type of feeling of fear protects us from potential harm and injury because it causes us to respond to and remove ourselves from potentially dangerous situations.

This is not the type of fear described in the Genesis story. Adam and Eve had no reason to feel afraid. They weren't under attack or threat of bodily harm. "Being afraid" is entirely different. It describes a state we too often live in. It's a state of anxiety or a lack of peace. It's a state of being unsettled and uncertain. This type of fear frequently dictates our decisions and our behavior in a negative way, causing us to live unfulfilled lives without meaningful impact. This type of fear is not the natural response to a potentially dangerous situation. Instead, it's a state of fear in response to our circumstances, perceptions, or decisions which hold us back from our potential. Adam and Eve made a poor decision. This decision caused guilt and shame, which led to irrational fear. This irrational fear then drove their behavior and decision-making, leading them into hiding and separation.

How many of us too often allow this to happen to ourselves? We develop irrational fears based on our circumstances or our pasts or our mistaken assumptions about others, and these fears then control our decisions and behaviors. When this happens, how we relate to others and to the world around us, in turn, becomes something far less fulfilling and impactful than it should be.

One of the world's greatest philosophers did his best to warn us against fear. In *The Phantom Menace* installment of the *Star Wars* trilogies, Yoda offers this wisdom: "Fear is the path to the dark side. Fear leads to anger. Anger leads to hate. Hate leads to suffering." Yoda is on to something profound. Our fears lead us to form assumptions, conclusions, and opinions about other people that often aren't true, but we believe nevertheless. As Yoda teaches, instead of intentionally choosing to love others, we develop anger and resentment. Not only does this lead to our own suffering, but it also prevents us from having a positive impact on others of which we are so capable when we refuse to let our fears drive our behavior.

If we take an honest look at those areas of our lives where we struggle the most, it's likely rooted in some sort of fear. There are so many different types of fear. Fear of the unknown. Fear of failure or even fear of success. Fear of what others think of us. Fear of what our future holds. Fear of people who look, act, and think differently than us. Fear of whether we will be taken care of or be able to provide for our families. Fear of change. Fear of what may happen to our children. Fear of things that are unfamiliar or which we don't understand.

I spent years caring way too much about what other people thought about me, or perhaps I should say fearing what others thought about me. I wanted to please people, and I wanted the affirmation people-pleasing provided. Now, Jenn tells me I may have swung the pendulum too far the other way, not caring enough about what others think. She may be right, which is an entirely different problem that also minimizes our potential impact. For now, let's focus on the fear issue. When I was younger, my concern with what others thought about me impacted how I lived and the decisions I made, and it certainly prevented me from having the impact I could have otherwise had. Sometimes I did things because others expected me to. Sometimes I didn't do things because others expected me not to. Either way, those concerns and fears drove me to self-centered decisions rather than action intentionally chosen out of love for others and a desire to positively impact others based on my unique gifts and talents and confidence in those giftings.

Letting our actions be controlled and driven by a state of fear, regardless of which particular fear is at the foundation, hinders and limits every aspect of our lives. Our relationships are less than they could be. Our jobs and careers are less meaningful, purposeful, and impactful. Our family lives don't flourish as much as possible. Our outputs and behaviors become about us and avoiding our fears instead of about loving and impacting others.

Returning to the faith-based foundation for leading a fearless life, we move from Adam and Eve's Genesis story, which first introduces us to fear, to the New Testament story of Jesus's birth. Many are familiar with the Christmas story. Jesus is born in a stable because his parents couldn't find a place to stay. An angel appeared to shepherds in a nearby field to announce Jesus's arrival. At least as recorded in scripture, the first words out of the angel's mouth were "be not afraid" (Luke 2:10 American Standard Version, *You Version*). Don't be afraid, because I'm bringing you good news.

I've never seen an angel, at least not that I'm aware of, but I think I'd be scared if I did. This would cause a healthy type of fear *feeling* we discussed above – the type which prompts us to remove ourselves from a dangerous situation to avoid danger. Therefore, it may seem the angel is simply telling the shepherds to calm down and not be scared because they weren't in any danger. Maybe that was part of the angel's intent. "Be not afraid," however, means something much deeper and more meaningful. In the story of Adam and Eve, the consequence of their decisions and actions is guilt and shame, which leads to fear, which in turn leads to hiding and separation. Jesus's arrival, on the other hand, ushered in a new message to "Be Not Afraid" because hope and joy have arrived and are available regardless of circumstances, situations, or past struggles and bad decisions.

This message to be not afraid, or fear not, or take courage, is repeated over and over again throughout the New Testament. This is the central and vital message of the Christian faith. Because of Jesus and who He is and what He did, then "be not afraid." However, even for those who don't claim this faith, there's a fundamental lesson to be embraced and adopted. Fear holds us back. Love and trust cast us forward. Whether we are a person of faith or without faith, embracing this fundamental truth is essential. When we love and trust instead of fear, real change and real impact happen.

Life is hard. It always has been, and it always will be. There are scary, bad, hard, challenging, and difficult things happening all around us. But there are also so many good and positive things happening, both in tiny doses and on a large scale. And if we want more of those good things in our lives, change is required. Something must shift and make room for it. Something new must lead us to it. The fears which hold us back must be replaced by love. We cannot be led by fear and expect to have the positive and lasting impact of which we are capable. This doesn't mean we don't have fears, but those fears must be overcome by and replaced with truth, hope, trust, and love.

There is something significant waiting for all of us if we recognize this fundamental need to change the way we interact with the world. Fear becomes love. Despair becomes joy. Death becomes life. Guilt and shame become forgiveness and freedom. When we intentionally choose to love others without fear, these things are possible without insecurity, without restriction, without distinction, without limits, and without whatever other rationalization or justification is holding us back. When we love hard, transformation happens. Restoration happens. Hearts are changed. Lives are altered. Instead of feeling like we are fighting *against* so many things, we suddenly find ourselves fighting *for* love, hope, peace, and joy. Those become a reality.

"Humans of New York" is a collection of stories based on interviews with thousands of people. Often these are interviews with people on the streets of New York. But sometimes they do other series. During a series of Rwandan stories, HONY told the story of a Rwandan pastor whose decision to love in the face of fear shows us what can be accomplished when we make this choice *despite* our fears. The events giving rise to this story occurred during the Rwandan Civil War of 1990, which involved the mass slaughter and genocide of over 800,000 Tutsi Rwandans (70% of the Tutsi population) by the Hutu majority government during a 100-day period.[56] The pastor described to Humans of New York how when the killings began, people came to his church for sanctuary. "I just kept bringing people inside the gate," he said, until over three hundred people were hiding on his property.[57] He filled as many hiding places as possible. Having heard he was hiding people, the militia arrived at his church carrying guns and machetes and demanding to come inside, but he "stood in the doorway and told them that they'd have to kill me first."[58] The group promised to return.

Soon, those in hiding ran out of food. Sleep was difficult, as they heard gunfire and screaming coming from the surrounding areas and believed they were next. After three weeks, a group of fifty killers returned, pushed past the pastor, and began pulling people from hiding places, dragging them outside and putting them in lines. The pastor recognized some of the killers, including some from his congregation, and began calling them by name. He asked them, "When I die, I am going to heaven. Where will you go?" [59] The killers began to argue with and threaten each other, none wanting to be the first to kill. Eventually, they ran off.

The pastor had not lost a single person. He said, "In the end, over three hundred people survived the genocide by hiding in this church. I can't remember all their faces. Life has taken us to many different corners. And some of them have left the country to begin new lives. But many of them still call me father." [60] He believes the genocide could have been stopped if more had taken a stand and used their influence. But most did nothing, offering different excuses, from being afraid to assuming the government was too powerful to oppose. But, according to this single pastor, "when you're standing aside while people die, every excuse is a lame one." [61]

I'm not sharing this story to show how we can be rescued from our difficult circumstances. Sometimes we receive rescue and protection. Sometimes we don't. Instead, I appreciate Humans of New York recording and sharing this story because it reveals the impact that can occur when we choose to "be not afraid" and love hard despite our fears. This pastor's decision to do that very thing changed lives. He chose the well-being of others over his own self-preservation, and he made an impact on the lives of those under his protection in ways they never forgot and likely passed on to others.

During my first two or three decades, the concept of loving hard was exactly that, a concept. It wasn't until I had a spouse and children that I truly understood sacrifice, devotion, and unconditional love. Loving the people around me hard requires all of these. It also requires that – even when the people in my life mess up, when they say or do things that don't reflect their good character, and when they make mistakes – I love them as hard as I can. Over time, I've slowly learned how to transform what was once a mere concept into daily practice. Jenn and my children, and everyone else in my life, no doubt wish I had figured it out sooner and didn't require so much practice. But I'm learning, and I'm trying.

Loving hard isn't easy. It's not supposed to be. Meaningful and lasting impact doesn't come from taking the simplest path. It comes from the difficult one. Many people in my life – family, friends, acquaintances, even perceived enemies – who have chosen intentionally to love me hard even in times of intense disagreement refuse to let our differences define us. Instead, they allow love to unite us. These intentional actions and choices give me hope. They prove that, perhaps, the frustration and discouragement I sometimes feel is misplaced and that we can in fact be better. We are better. I cannot overstate the positive and lasting impact these individuals have on me when they choose to love hard. It inspires me to do the same for others, and our collective impact compounds.

We become the light. And light shines in the darkness. No matter how small, this beacon brings encouragement and hope. May we all be light in the world around us by loving others hard. And by so doing, may we bring hope to every circumstance and relationship, no matter how difficult they may be.

Endnotes

1   "Love: Definition of Love by Oxford Dictionary on Lexico.com." *Lexico Dictionaries | English*, Lexico Dictionaries, https://www.lexico.com/definition/love. Accessed 23 Sept. 2020.

2   "Love." https://www.lexico.com/definition/love.

3   Rinehart, Nathaniel. "NEEDTOBREATHE – HARD LOVE Lyrics | AZLyrics.com." *AZ Lyrics*, 2020, www.azlyrics.com/lyrics/needtobreathe/hardlove.html.

4   CS Lewis Quotes (84 Quotes)." *Goodreads*, Goodreads, 23 Sept. 2020, www.goodreads.com/quotes/19964-i-didn-t-go-to-religion-to-make-me-happy-i.

5   "Perspective: Definition of Perspective by Oxford Dictionary on Lexico.com," *Lexico Dictionaries | English*, Lexico Dictionaries, https://www.lexico.com/definition/perspective. Accessed 23 Sept. 2020.

6   http://www.wingclips.com/movie-clips/the-great-outdoors/i-see-trees.

7   Wallis, Jim. *God's Politics: Why the Right Gets It Wrong and the Left Doesn't Get It*. HarperCollins, 2005, p. 347-48.

8   "In U.S., Decline of Christianity Continues at Rapid Pace." *Pew Research Center's Religion & Public Life Project*, 17 Oct. 2019, www.pewforum.org/2019/10/17/in-u-s-decline-of-christianity-continues-at-rapid-pace/.

9   "In U.S., Decline of Christianity Continues at Rapid Pace." *Pew Research Center's Religion & Public Life Project*, 17 Oct. 2019.

10 Cox, Daniel, and Amelia Thomson-DeVeaux. "Millennials Are Leaving Religion And Not Coming Back." *FiveThirtyEight*, FiveThirtyEight, 12 Dec. 2019, fivethirtyeight.com/features/millennials-are-leaving-religion-and-not-coming-back/.

11 Goff, Bob. *Live in Grace, Walk in Love.* Nelson Books, an Imprint of Thomas Nelson, 2019, p. 663.

12 Wenger, Chester. "An Open Letter to My Beloved Church." *Anabaptist World*, 6 Nov. 2014, themennonite.org/opinion/open-letter-beloved-church/.

13 Wenger, Chester. "An Open Letter to My Beloved Church." *Anabaptist World*, 6 Nov. 2014.

14 Wenger, Chester. "An Open Letter to My Beloved Church." *Anabaptist World*, 6 Nov. 2014.

15 "Identity: Definition of Identity by Oxford Dictionary on Lexico. com." *Lexico Dictionaries | English*, Lexico Dictionaries, https://www.lexico.com/definition/identity. Accessed 23 Sept. 2020.

16 "Testimonials." *Acts 4 Others*, 24 Sept. 2020, www.acts4others. org/testimonials.

17 "Purpose: Definition of Purpose by Oxford Dictionary on Lexico. com." *Lexico Dictionaries | English*, Lexico Dictionaries, https://www.lexico.com/definition/purpose. Accessed 23 Sept. 2020.

18 Wright, N. T. *Surprised by Hope: Rethinking Heaven, the Resurrection, and the Mission of the Church.* HarperOne, an Imprint of HarperCollins Publishers, 2018.

19 Holcomb, Drew. "Drew Holcomb & The Neighbors - Good Light Lyrics ..." *AZ Lyrics*, 2020, www.azlyrics.com/lyrics/drewholcombtheneighbors/goodlight.html.

20 "The One Where Phoebe Hates PBS." *Friends.* NBC. Oct. 15, 1998. Television.

21 Husain, Mishal. "Malala: The girl who was shot for going to school." *BBC News*, BBC, 7 Oct. 2013, https://www.bbc.com/news/magazine-24379018.

22 Husain, Mishal. "Malala: The girl who was shot for going to school." *BBC News*, 7 Oct. 2013.

23 "Senate Stories: The Caning of Senator Charles Sumner." *U.S. Senate: The Caning of Senator Charles Sumner,* 4 May 2020, https://www.senate.gov/artandhistory/history/minute/The_Caning_of_Senator_Charles_Sumner.htm.

24 "The Most Infamous Floor Brawl in the History of the U.S. House of Representatives." *US House of Representatives: History, Art & Archives,* https://history.house.gov/Historical-Highlights/1851-1900/The-most-infamous-floor-brawl-in-the-history-of-the-U-S--House-of-Representatives/. Accessed Sept. 23, 2020.

25 Little, Becky. "Violence in Congress Before the Civil War: From Canings and Stabbings to Murder." *History.com*, A&E Television Networks, 24 July 2019, www.history.com/news/charles-sumner-caning-cilley-duel-congressional-violence.

26 "Representative Roger Griswold of Connecticut Attacked Matthew Lyon of Vermont on the House Floor." *US House of Representatives: History, Art & Archives*, history.house.gov/Historical-Highlights/1700s/Representative-Roger-Griswold-of-Connecticut-attacked-Matthew-Lyon-of-Vermont-on-the-House-Floor/. Accessed Sept. 23, 2020.

27 Romano, Lois. "Duel on the Hill." *The Washington Post*, WP Company, 6 Mar. 1985, www.washingtonpost.com/archive/lifestyle/1985/03/06/duel-on-the-hill/a66a3746-68c3-471a-8314-c9a30390dd46/.

28 Itkowitz, Colby. "The Health 202: Patrick Kennedy Shepherded a Major Mental-Health Bill into Law. Ten Years Later, Big Barriers Remain." *The Washington Post*, WP Company, 4 Oct. 2018, www.washingtonpost.com/news/powerpost/paloma/the-health-202/2018/10/04/the-health-202-patrick-kennedy-shepherded-a-major-mental-hill-bill-into-law-ten-years-later-big-barriers-remain/5bb510121b326b7c8a8d17f5/.

29 Wren, Jennifer. *Facebook,* 2 June 2020, https://www.facebook.com/jennifer.h.wren.

30 "History of Bipartisanship." *Bipartisan Policy Center*, 23 Sept. 2020, bipartisanpolicy.org/history-of-bipartisanship.

31 "History of Bipartisanship." *Bipartisan Policy Center.* 23 Sept. 2020.

32 "History of Bipartisanship." *Bipartisan Policy Center.* 23 Sept. 2020.

33 Penrose, Krystal. "8 Lessons From Brene Brown On Healing Through Grief." *FuneralOne Blog*, 4 Sept. 2019, blog.funeralone.com/grief-and-healing/brene-brown-grief/.

34 "The Heart of Leadership." *The John Maxwell Team*, 24 Sept. 2020, johnmaxwellteam.com/the-heart-of-leadership/.

35 "A Tale of Two Championships." *Center for Sports Leadership and Innovation*, 31 Oct. 2018, sportsleadership.utexas.edu/longhorn-tribune/a-tale-of-two-championships-by-mack-brown/.

36 "A Tale of Two Championships." *Center for Sports Leadership and Innovation.* 31 Oct. 2018.

37 DeCock, Luke. "After Mack Brown Won over the Hearts and Minds of UNC's Players, the Wins Followed." *Newsobserver*, Ra-

leigh News & Observer, 28 Dec. 2019, www.newsobserver.com/
sports/spt-columns-blogs/luke-decock/article238751863.html.

38   Hyatt, Michael. "7 Suggestions for Asking More Powerful Questions."
Michael Hyatt, 10 July 2019, michaelhyatt.com/asking-more-power-
ful-questions/.

39   "Doris Kearns Goodwin." *Pittsburgh Arts & Lectures*, 30 Oct. 2019,
pittsburghlectures.org/lectures/doris-kearns-goodwin/.

40   Caramela, Sammi. "Mary Parker Follett's Management Theory."
Business.com, Business.com, 21 Feb. 2018, www.business.com/
articles/management-theory-of-mary-parker-follett/.

41   Brookhiser, Richard. "In 'Friends Divided,' John Adams and Thomas
Jefferson Beg to Differ." *The New York Times*, The New York Times,
31 Oct. 2017, www.nytimes.com/2017/10/31/books/review/friends-
divided-john-adams-thomas-jefferson-gordon-s-wood.html.

42   Brookhiser, Richard. "In 'Friends Divided,' John Adams and
Thomas Jefferson Beg to Differ." *The New York Times*, 31 Oct. 2017.

43   Brookhiser, Richard. "In 'Friends Divided,' John Adams and Thomas
Jefferson Beg to Differ." *The New York Times*, 31 Oct. 2017.

44   Eldridge, Charles. "Every Day Is Easter Sunday." *Lewistownsen-
tinel.com*, 18 Apr. 2020, www.lewistownsentinel.com/news/reli-
gion/2020/04/every-day-is-easter-sunday/.

45   Eldridge, Charles. "Every Day is Easter Sunday." *Lewistownsenti-
nel.com*, 18 Apr. 2020.

46   Eldridge, Charles. "Every Day is Easter Sunday." *Lewistownsenti-
nel.com*, 18 Apr. 2020.

47   @bobgoff (Bob Goff). "The way we treat people we disagree with
the most is a report card on what we've learned about love."
Twitter, 28 June 2015, 10:32 a.m.

48   Mindvalley. "What's The Difference Between Joy Vs Happiness?"
Mindvalley Blog, 1 Jan. 2019, blog.mindvalley.com/joy-vs-happiness/.

49   Mindvalley. "What's The Difference Between Joy Vs Happiness?"
Mindvalley Blog, 1 Jan. 2019, blog.mindvalley.com/joy-vs-happiness/.

50   Lewis, C.S. "A Quote by C.S. Lewis." *Goodreads*, Goodreads, www.
goodreads.com/quotes/31889-i-sometimes-wonder-if-all-plea-
sures-are-not-substitutes-for. Accessed Sept. 24, 2020.

51   Emory Report. "What the Declaration of Independence Really
Means by 'Pursuit of Happiness'." *Emory University | Atlanta,
GA*, 3 July 2018, news.emory.edu/stories/2014/06/er_pursuit_of_
happiness/campus.html.

52 Emory Report. "What the Declaration of Independence Really Means by 'Pursuit of Happiness'." news.emory.edu/stories/2014/06/er_pursuit_of_happiness/campus.html.

53 Gettleman, Jeffrey, et al. "A Man's Last Letter Before Being Killed on a Forbidden Island." *The New York Times*, The New York Times, 23 Nov. 2018, www.nytimes.com/2018/11/23/world/asia/andaman-missionary-john-chau.html.

54 Gettleman, *et al.*, "A Man's Last Letter Before Being Killed on a Forbidden Island." *The New York Times*, 23 Nov. 2018.

55 Genesis 3:8-10.

56 Bhalla, Nita. "Rwanda Remembers 800,000 Killed on 25th Anniversary of Genocide." *News.trust.org*, 6 Apr. 2019, news.trust.org/item/20190406150007-ol1v2/.

57 Humansofnewyork. "Humansofnewyork." *Humans of New York*, 16 Oct. 2018, www.humansofnewyork.com/post/179120698766/%C2%BC-first-came-the-meetings-they-were-openly.

58 Humansofnewyork. "Humansofnewyork." *Humans of New York*, 17 Oct. 2018, www.humansofnewyork.com/post/179125452651/24-we-filled-every-hiding-place-with-a-person.

59 Humansofnewyork. "Humansofnewyork." *Humans of New York*, 17 Oct. 2018, www.humansofnewyork.com/post/179128952456/%C2%BE-the-next-time-the-killers-came-there-were.

60 Humansofnewyork. "Humansofnewyork." *Humans of New York*, 17 Oct. 2018, www.humansofnewyork.com/post/179129392811/44-we-didnt-lose-a-single-person-after.

61 Humansofnewyork. "Humansofnewyork." *Humans of New York*, 17 Oct. 2018, www.humansofnewyork.com/post/179129392811/44-we-didnt-lose-a-single-person-after.

CPSIA information can be obtained
at www.ICGtesting.com
Printed in the USA
LVHW090233070421
683679LV00006B/84